Copyright © 2023 by Herman Strange (Author)
All rights reserved. This book or any portion thereof may not be reproduced or used in any manner whatsoever without the express written permission of the publisher except for the use of brief quotations in a book review.

This book is copyright protected. This is only for personal use. You cannot amend, distributor, sell, use, quote or paraphrase any part or the content within this book without the consent of the author. Please note the information contained within this document is for educational and entertainment purposes only. Every attempt has been made to provide accurate, up to date and reliable complete information. No warranties of any kind are expressed or implied.

Readers acknowledge that the author is not engaging in the rendering of legal, financial, medical or professional advice. The content of this book has been derived from various sources. Please consult a licensed professional before attempting any techniques outlined in this book.

By reading this document, the readers agree that under no circumstances are the author responsible for any losses, direct or indirect, which are incurred as a result of the use of information contained within this document, including but not limited to errors, omissions or inaccuracies.

Thank you very much for reading this book.

Title: Beyond the Decentralized Dream-Navigating the Pitfalls of Blockchain Adoption in Supply Chain Subtitle: Lessons Learned from Real-World Implementations

**Series: Blockchain and Cryptocurrency Exposed
Author: Herman Strange**

Table of Contents

Introduction 6
   Overview of blockchain technology 6
   Importance of supply chain management 8
   Benefits and risks of adopting blockchain technology in supply chain management 9

Chapter 1: Technical Challenges 11
   Complexity and cost of implementation 11
   Limited scalability of blockchain networks 13
   Lack of interoperability between different blockchain networks 15
   Dependence on technology and potential for system failures . 17
   Energy consumption and environmental concerns 19
   Integration challenges with legacy systems and processes 21

Chapter 2: Security Challenges 23
   Potential vulnerabilities and security risks 23
   Lack of regulation and legal challenges 25
   Risks associated with data privacy and confidentiality 26
   51% attack and network consensus issues 28
   Centralization risks with private blockchains 30
   Potential for smart contract errors and vulnerabilities 32

Chapter 3: Organizational Challenges 35
   Resistance to change and lack of buy-in from stakeholders ... 35
   Limited functionality of blockchain technology in supply chain management 37

    Limited standardization and fragmentation of blockchain networks 39
    Difficulty of implementation and need for specialized expertise 42
    Challenges in managing and maintaining decentralized networks 45
    Ethical and social implications of blockchain technology 50

Chapter 4: Financial Challenges 52
    High cost of implementing and maintaining blockchain technology 52
    Limited return on investment for some organizations 54
    Challenges associated with pricing and revenue models 56
    Difficulty in measuring and proving ROI 59
    Challenges in securing funding for blockchain projects 61
    Challenges in achieving cost efficiencies and scale 64

Chapter 5: Legal and Regulatory Challenges 67
    Lack of clear legal framework and regulatory guidance 67
    Potential liability and compliance risks 69
    Challenges associated with intellectual property and ownership rights 72
    Implications of cross-border transactions and international regulations 75
    Implications of blockchain-based smart contracts on contract law 79
    Potential for blockchain technology to facilitate illegal activities 81

Chapter 6: Ethical and Social Challenges 83

Potential for blockchain technology to exacerbate existing power imbalances 83
Implications for data privacy and surveillance 89
Potential for discrimination and bias in smart contracts 91
Potential for environmental harm and inequality 94
Potential for blockchain technology to facilitate unethical or illegal activities 98
Ethical and social implications of blockchain-based supply chain traceability 101

Conclusion 105
Summary of key points 105
Strategies for mitigating the risks and challenges of adopting blockchain technology in supply chain management 107
Future outlook for blockchain technology in the supply chain 109

Potential References 112

Introduction
Overview of blockchain technology

The concept of blockchain technology was first introduced in 2008 as a means to create a decentralized digital currency, Bitcoin. However, it has since evolved to become a versatile technology that has the potential to transform many industries, including supply chain management.

At its core, blockchain is a distributed ledger technology that enables secure, transparent, and tamper-proof transactions without the need for intermediaries such as banks or other financial institutions. Each transaction is recorded in a block, which is linked to the previous block to form a chain of blocks. This creates a permanent and immutable record of all transactions, which can be verified by anyone on the network.

One of the key features of blockchain is its decentralized nature. Instead of having a central authority to verify transactions, blockchain relies on a network of nodes that work together to validate transactions and maintain the integrity of the ledger. This makes it more secure and less susceptible to hacking or fraud.

Another important aspect of blockchain is its use of cryptography to ensure the privacy and security of transactions. Each user has a unique cryptographic key that is used to sign transactions, and all transactions are verified by consensus among the nodes on the network. This makes it difficult for anyone to alter or tamper with the ledger without being detected.

In addition to its security and decentralization features, blockchain also has the potential to facilitate automation, transparency, and efficiency in supply chain management. By using blockchain to track products and shipments, companies can ensure that goods are delivered to the right place at the right time, and that all parties involved in the supply chain have access to real-time information about the status of the shipment.

Despite its potential benefits, however, blockchain is not without its challenges and limitations. As we will discuss in this book, there are several technical, security, organizational, financial, legal, and ethical challenges that must be addressed before blockchain can be fully adopted in supply chain management.

Overall, the use of blockchain technology in supply chain management has the potential to revolutionize the way goods are produced, distributed, and consumed. However, it is important to be aware of the challenges and risks associated with its adoption, in order to navigate the pitfalls and ensure a successful implementation.

Importance of supply chain management

The supply chain is a critical component of any business, encompassing all the activities involved in the creation and delivery of goods or services to customers. Effective supply chain management is essential to ensure that products are produced and delivered to customers on time, at the right cost, and with the desired level of quality. Supply chain management also involves managing risks, ensuring compliance with regulations, and improving sustainability.

Supply chain management is becoming increasingly important in today's globalized economy, with companies facing greater competition, shorter product life cycles, and more complex supply chains. Consumers are also becoming more demanding, expecting faster delivery times, greater product variety, and higher levels of service.

Blockchain technology has the potential to transform supply chain management by providing greater transparency, security, and efficiency. By using a decentralized and distributed ledger, blockchain can enable secure and transparent tracking of products from the point of origin to the end customer. This can help to reduce fraud, counterfeiting, and supply chain disruptions, while also improving trust and collaboration between supply chain partners.

Given the importance of supply chain management, and the potential benefits of blockchain technology, it is no surprise that many companies are exploring the use of blockchain in their supply chains. However, as we will explore in this book, there are also many challenges and risks associated with adopting blockchain technology in the supply chain. These challenges range from technical and security issues to organizational, financial, and legal challenges. Therefore, it is important to carefully consider the benefits and risks of blockchain adoption in the supply chain, and to develop strategies for mitigating these risks.

Benefits and risks of adopting blockchain technology in supply chain management

Benefits and risks of adopting blockchain technology in supply chain management

Blockchain technology has the potential to revolutionize supply chain management by improving transparency, security, and efficiency. However, like any emerging technology, blockchain adoption in the supply chain also poses significant risks and challenges that organizations need to consider before implementation.

Benefits:

1. Transparency: Blockchain technology provides a transparent and immutable record of transactions and data. This allows for enhanced traceability and accountability in the supply chain, which can help to prevent fraud, reduce waste, and improve efficiency.

2. Security: Blockchain technology uses advanced encryption and consensus mechanisms to ensure the security and integrity of data. This can help to reduce the risk of cyber attacks, data breaches, and other security threats in the supply chain.

3. Efficiency: Blockchain technology has the potential to streamline supply chain processes by reducing the need for intermediaries and manual data entry. This can help to reduce costs, increase speed, and improve overall efficiency.

4. Trust: Blockchain technology can help to establish trust between parties in the supply chain by providing a shared and verifiable record of transactions and data. This can help to reduce disputes, improve collaboration, and enhance relationships between supply chain partners.

Risks:

1. Complexity: Blockchain technology is complex and requires specialized knowledge and expertise to implement and maintain. This can make it difficult for organizations to adopt and integrate blockchain into their existing supply chain systems.

2. Scalability: Blockchain technology is still in its early stages of development and is not yet capable of handling the volume and complexity of transactions required in large-scale supply chain operations. This can limit the scalability and practicality of blockchain adoption in the supply chain.

3. Interoperability: There are currently multiple blockchain platforms and networks, each with their own protocols and standards. This lack of interoperability can make it difficult for organizations to integrate blockchain into their existing supply chain systems.

4. Cost: The cost of implementing and maintaining blockchain technology can be high, especially for small and medium-sized enterprises. This can limit the accessibility and affordability of blockchain adoption in the supply chain.

5. Regulation: The legal and regulatory framework for blockchain technology is still developing, which can create uncertainty and risk for organizations considering blockchain adoption in the supply chain.

Overall, while there are significant benefits to adopting blockchain technology in the supply chain, organizations need to carefully consider the risks and challenges before implementation. A thorough understanding of the technology, its potential applications, and the regulatory environment is critical for successful blockchain adoption in the supply chain.

Chapter 1: Technical Challenges
Complexity and cost of implementation

Complexity and cost of implementation is one of the major technical challenges in adopting blockchain technology in supply chain management. While blockchain has the potential to bring transparency, traceability, and security to supply chain operations, implementing the technology can be complex and costly.

One of the main reasons for the complexity and cost of implementation is the distributed nature of blockchain networks. Unlike centralized systems, blockchain networks require multiple nodes to validate and record transactions, which can result in increased complexity and cost. In addition, implementing blockchain technology may require significant changes to existing supply chain systems and processes, which can add to the complexity and cost of the implementation.

Another factor contributing to the complexity and cost of implementation is the need for specialized expertise. Blockchain technology is still relatively new and requires specialized knowledge and skills to implement effectively. This can add to the cost of implementation, as organizations may need to hire experts or consultants to assist with the implementation.

Furthermore, the cost of implementing blockchain technology can be high due to the need for specialized hardware and software. For example, mining hardware is required for proof-of-work blockchain networks, which can be costly to acquire and maintain. In addition, blockchain software and development tools may also come at a premium, adding to the overall cost of implementation.

To mitigate the complexity and cost of implementation, organizations may need to take a phased approach to adopting blockchain technology in their supply chains. This approach may involve starting with smaller, low-risk projects and gradually scaling up over time. It may also involve partnering with other organizations or industry groups to share the cost and expertise required for implementation.

Overall, while the complexity and cost of implementation can be a significant challenge in adopting blockchain technology in supply chain management, the potential benefits may outweigh the costs in the long run. By addressing these challenges through careful planning, collaboration, and phased implementation, organizations can successfully adopt blockchain technology and improve their supply chain operations.

Limited scalability of blockchain networks

Blockchain technology is often touted for its potential to revolutionize supply chain management by enabling greater transparency, efficiency, and security. However, one of the biggest technical challenges that organizations face when adopting blockchain for supply chain management is limited scalability.

Blockchain networks operate by validating and recording transactions across a decentralized network of computers, or nodes. Each node in the network maintains a copy of the blockchain ledger, and any changes to the ledger must be verified by consensus among the nodes. This consensus mechanism helps to ensure the integrity and security of the blockchain, but it also creates a bottleneck for scalability.

As more transactions are added to the blockchain, the size of the ledger grows, and the time required to verify new transactions and reach consensus increases. This can result in slower transaction processing times, increased costs, and reduced overall efficiency.

One of the key factors that limit the scalability of blockchain networks is the size of the blocks that make up the blockchain. Blocks are batches of transactions that are verified and added to the ledger. Most blockchain networks have a fixed block size, which can limit the number of transactions that can be processed within a given timeframe.

To address the issue of limited scalability, blockchain developers have explored a range of solutions, including increasing block size, optimizing consensus mechanisms, and using off-chain transactions. However, each solution comes with its own trade-offs and challenges.

Increasing block size can improve scalability, but it can also increase the risk of centralization, as larger blocks require more computing power and storage capacity to process and validate. Optimizing consensus mechanisms can also improve scalability, but it may require significant changes to the underlying blockchain protocol and could impact the security and integrity of the blockchain.

Off-chain transactions, which allow certain transactions to be processed outside of the blockchain, can also help to improve scalability. However, they introduce new complexities and require additional infrastructure and governance.

Overall, limited scalability remains a significant technical challenge for organizations seeking to adopt blockchain for supply chain management. To successfully navigate this challenge, organizations will need to carefully consider their specific use case and explore a range of solutions and trade-offs.

Lack of interoperability between different blockchain networks

One of the key technical challenges facing the adoption of blockchain technology in supply chain management is the lack of interoperability between different blockchain networks. Interoperability refers to the ability of different blockchain networks to communicate and exchange data seamlessly, regardless of their underlying protocols or design.

Currently, there are many different blockchain networks in operation, each with their own unique design and protocols. Some of these networks are public, while others are private or permissioned. While each of these networks may offer unique benefits for supply chain management, they typically operate in silos, making it difficult for data and information to flow freely between them.

This lack of interoperability presents a significant challenge for supply chain management, as it can limit the ability of organizations to share data and collaborate effectively. For example, a company that uses a private blockchain network to manage its internal supply chain processes may struggle to share data with a partner that uses a public blockchain network.

There are several factors contributing to the lack of interoperability in the blockchain ecosystem. One of the main reasons is the lack of standardization in the industry. Different blockchain networks use different protocols and standards, making it difficult to achieve seamless interoperability. Moreover, many of the existing blockchain networks were not designed with interoperability in mind, as their primary focus was on security, privacy, and other features.

There have been several efforts to address the lack of interoperability in the blockchain ecosystem. One approach is to develop common standards and protocols that can be used across different blockchain networks. For example, the InterWork Alliance (IWA) is a non-profit organization that is working to develop a common framework for interoperability between different blockchain networks.

Another approach is to use middleware or bridging technologies that can translate data and transactions between different blockchain networks. For example, the Cosmos Network is a project that aims to create an interoperable network of blockchains by using a middleware layer to enable communication between different networks.

Overall, the lack of interoperability between different blockchain networks is a significant challenge for the adoption of blockchain technology in supply chain management. However, there are several initiatives underway to address this challenge, and it is likely that interoperability will improve over time as the industry matures.

Dependence on technology and potential for system failures

Dependence on technology and potential for system failures are significant challenges associated with the adoption of blockchain technology in supply chain management. While blockchain networks are designed to be decentralized and resistant to tampering, they are still reliant on underlying technologies such as computer hardware, software, and internet connectivity.

One of the primary concerns regarding the dependence on technology is the potential for system failures. If a blockchain network experiences a technical issue, such as a software bug or hardware failure, it could result in the loss of critical data or the disruption of supply chain operations. Additionally, since blockchain networks rely on a consensus mechanism to validate transactions, any technical issue that affects the network's ability to reach consensus could result in a loss of trust in the system and a significant disruption to the supply chain.

Another challenge associated with the dependence on technology is the need for ongoing maintenance and support. While blockchain networks are designed to be self-sustaining and automated, they still require regular updates, maintenance, and monitoring to ensure their ongoing security and functionality. This can be costly and time-consuming, particularly for organizations that lack the necessary expertise and resources.

Moreover, the dependence on technology also raises concerns about the potential for hacking and cyber-attacks. Blockchain networks are not immune to hacking and cyber-attacks, and any successful attack on the network could result in significant financial losses and reputational damage for the organizations involved.

To mitigate these challenges, organizations adopting blockchain technology in supply chain management need to carefully consider the underlying technology and infrastructure needed to support the network. They should also implement robust security measures, such as multi-factor authentication and regular vulnerability assessments, to ensure the network's ongoing security and resilience. Finally, organizations should establish contingency plans and disaster recovery procedures to mitigate the risks associated with system failures and cyber-attacks.

Energy consumption and environmental concerns

One of the most significant technical challenges associated with blockchain technology is its high energy consumption and environmental impact. The process of verifying transactions on a blockchain network requires a vast amount of computing power, which translates into high energy consumption.

According to some estimates, the Bitcoin network, which is the most well-known and widely used blockchain network, consumes more energy than entire countries such as Argentina or the Netherlands. This is because the mining process of Bitcoin, which involves solving complex mathematical problems to validate transactions and add them to the blockchain ledger, requires an enormous amount of computational power.

The high energy consumption of blockchain networks has raised concerns about their environmental impact. The carbon footprint of blockchain technology is significant, with some reports suggesting that the energy consumption of blockchain networks is equivalent to the annual energy consumption of some small countries.

Another issue is the e-waste generated by the use of specialized hardware required to mine cryptocurrencies. As the computing power required to validate transactions on the blockchain network increases, miners must continuously upgrade their hardware to remain competitive. This leads to a significant amount of electronic waste generated, which poses a threat to the environment.

Despite the concerns about the energy consumption and environmental impact of blockchain technology, some researchers argue that blockchain technology can actually help promote environmental sustainability. For example, blockchain-based systems can be used to track the origin and movement of goods, which can help reduce the carbon footprint of supply chains. By using blockchain technology, organizations can track the movement of goods from the point of origin to the point of consumption, allowing them to identify and address inefficiencies in the supply chain that contribute to carbon emissions.

Overall, the energy consumption and environmental impact of blockchain technology are significant technical challenges that must be addressed. While blockchain technology can have positive impacts on environmental sustainability, its high energy consumption and e-waste generation cannot be ignored. As the use of blockchain technology in supply chain management continues to grow, it is essential to find ways to reduce its energy consumption and minimize its environmental impact.

Integration challenges with legacy systems and processes

Blockchain technology has been around for over a decade, but many industries and organizations are still reliant on legacy systems and processes. Integrating blockchain technology with these systems can be a significant challenge, and there are several potential roadblocks that organizations may encounter.

One of the main challenges of integrating blockchain technology with legacy systems is the need for significant technical expertise. Many legacy systems were designed and implemented years ago, and the staff responsible for maintaining them may not have experience with newer technologies like blockchain. This can lead to delays and increased costs as organizations bring in outside consultants or invest in training their staff.

Another challenge is the need for data standardization. Blockchain technology relies on data being recorded in a standardized format, but legacy systems may have different data structures and naming conventions. This can make it difficult to integrate data from different sources, which can in turn hinder the effectiveness of blockchain-based supply chain management.

There are also challenges related to the differences in processing speeds and data storage requirements between blockchain and legacy systems. Legacy systems may have different requirements for processing speeds and data storage, which can affect how quickly data can be verified and stored on the blockchain. This can create bottlenecks and delays, particularly if organizations are relying on blockchain technology to process high volumes of transactions.

Finally, there are potential security risks associated with integrating blockchain technology with legacy systems. Legacy systems may not have the same security features and protocols as blockchain, which can make them vulnerable to cyberattacks and other security breaches. Organizations need to be aware of these risks and take steps to mitigate them, such as implementing robust access controls and monitoring systems.

Overall, integration challenges with legacy systems and processes can be a significant hurdle for organizations looking to adopt blockchain technology in supply chain management. Organizations need to be aware of these challenges and take steps to overcome them, such as investing in staff training, standardizing data formats, and implementing robust security measures. By doing so, they can unlock the benefits of blockchain technology and drive innovation in their supply chain management processes.

Chapter 2: Security Challenges
Potential vulnerabilities and security risks

As with any technology, blockchain networks are not immune to security risks and vulnerabilities. In fact, the decentralized nature of blockchain technology can create unique security challenges.

One of the most significant security risks associated with blockchain technology is the potential for a 51% attack. In a proof-of-work blockchain network, a 51% attack occurs when a single entity or group of entities controls more than 51% of the network's computing power. With this level of control, the attacker could potentially manipulate the blockchain by preventing transactions, reversing transactions, and even double-spending coins. While the likelihood of a 51% attack occurring on a well-established blockchain network like Bitcoin is low, smaller and newer networks are more vulnerable to this type of attack.

Another security risk associated with blockchain technology is the potential for smart contract vulnerabilities. Smart contracts are self-executing contracts with the terms of the agreement between buyer and seller being directly written into lines of code. These contracts are stored on the blockchain, allowing for automated execution without the need for intermediaries. However, if the code is poorly written or contains vulnerabilities, it can be exploited by attackers, resulting in financial loss or other damages. In recent years, there have been several high-profile cases of smart contract vulnerabilities, including the DAO hack in 2016.

Blockchain networks can also be vulnerable to traditional security threats, such as hacking, malware, and phishing attacks. While the decentralized nature of blockchain technology can provide some level of protection against these threats, it is not immune to them. Additionally, the lack of regulation and oversight in the blockchain industry can make it difficult to hold attackers accountable and recover lost funds.

Furthermore, the lack of regulation and legal challenges can create additional security risks in the blockchain industry. Without clear legal frameworks and regulatory guidance, businesses may struggle to navigate complex legal issues related to blockchain technology. This can create opportunities for bad actors to exploit legal loopholes and engage in fraudulent activities.

In summary, while blockchain technology has the potential to enhance security in supply chain management, it also presents unique security challenges. To mitigate these risks, businesses must carefully consider the security implications of blockchain adoption and implement appropriate security measures. These measures may include conducting thorough security audits of smart contracts, implementing strong access controls, and regularly monitoring blockchain networks for potential threats.

Lack of regulation and legal challenges

The lack of clear regulatory frameworks for blockchain technology in supply chain management can present legal challenges for organizations. Since the technology is still relatively new and constantly evolving, regulatory bodies may struggle to keep up with the pace of innovation and issue clear guidelines for compliance.

In addition, the decentralized and immutable nature of blockchain can make it difficult to resolve disputes or enforce legal agreements. The absence of a central authority or intermediary can make it challenging to identify responsible parties in case of fraud or other illegal activities. This can make it difficult for organizations to protect their assets and intellectual property, as well as ensure compliance with data privacy regulations.

Furthermore, the use of blockchain technology in supply chain management can raise legal questions around ownership and liability. Smart contracts, which are self-executing agreements that automatically trigger when specific conditions are met, can make it difficult to assign responsibility for errors or damages. This is especially true in cases where smart contracts are used to govern complex supply chain processes involving multiple parties, such as shipping and customs clearance.

In order to address these legal challenges, it is important for organizations to stay up-to-date on regulatory developments and work closely with legal counsel to ensure compliance. They may also need to consider alternative dispute resolution mechanisms, such as arbitration, to resolve disputes in a timely and efficient manner. Additionally, organizations may need to develop new governance structures and contractual frameworks to ensure that legal and regulatory requirements are met.

Risks associated with data privacy and confidentiality

The use of blockchain technology in supply chain management raises a number of concerns about data privacy and confidentiality. While blockchain technology is designed to be secure and immutable, there are still risks associated with the exposure of sensitive information to unauthorized parties.

One of the primary risks associated with data privacy and confidentiality is the potential for data breaches. Blockchain networks are often used to store sensitive information, such as customer data, financial information, and trade secrets. If this information is not properly secured, it could be vulnerable to attacks by malicious actors.

Another risk associated with data privacy and confidentiality is the potential for data leakage. This can occur when sensitive information is inadvertently shared with unauthorized parties, either through human error or through vulnerabilities in the blockchain network itself.

In addition to these risks, there is also a concern about the potential for data manipulation. Because blockchain networks are decentralized and rely on a consensus mechanism to validate transactions, there is a risk that malicious actors could manipulate the data stored on the network to their advantage.

To mitigate these risks, organizations must take steps to ensure that their blockchain networks are properly secured and that sensitive information is only accessible to authorized parties. This can include implementing strong access controls, using encryption to protect sensitive data, and regularly monitoring the network for any suspicious activity.

Another important consideration is the use of smart contracts, which can automate a wide range of supply chain transactions. While smart contracts can be highly efficient and effective, they also raise a number of concerns about data privacy and confidentiality. For example, if a smart contract is designed to automatically execute a transaction based on a specific set of conditions, there is a risk that the conditions themselves could be used to compromise the privacy of sensitive information.

To address these concerns, organizations must carefully consider the design and implementation of their smart contracts, ensuring that they are properly secured and that sensitive information is only accessible to authorized parties. They must also ensure that their smart contracts are compliant with relevant data privacy regulations and that they have appropriate policies and procedures in place to govern their use.

In addition to these technical considerations, organizations must also take steps to address the human factor in data privacy and confidentiality. This can include implementing training and awareness programs for employees, as well as establishing clear policies and procedures for the handling of sensitive information.

Overall, while blockchain technology offers many benefits for supply chain management, it also raises a number of concerns about data privacy and confidentiality. By taking a proactive and comprehensive approach to addressing these concerns, organizations can ensure that they are able to leverage the full potential of blockchain technology while minimizing the risks associated with its use.

51% attack and network consensus issues

Blockchain technology is built upon the principles of decentralization and immutability, which makes it a secure platform for data storage and transaction processing. However, this security is not absolute, and blockchain networks are still vulnerable to certain types of attacks. One of the most significant security risks associated with blockchain is the 51% attack.

A 51% attack, also known as a majority attack or a double-spend attack, occurs when a single entity or group of entities controls more than 50% of the computing power on a blockchain network. This gives them the ability to manipulate the network and potentially cause irreparable harm to the blockchain.

The primary goal of a 51% attack is to create a fork in the blockchain, which allows the attacker to double-spend their digital assets. In a double-spend attack, the attacker sends a transaction to a recipient, and then immediately sends the same assets to themselves on another block on the blockchain. Since the attacker controls the majority of the network's computing power, they can manipulate the network's consensus mechanism and ensure that their transaction is accepted by the network. This essentially allows the attacker to spend the same digital assets twice, which can have significant financial implications for the affected parties.

The potential consequences of a 51% attack can be severe, as it can undermine the integrity of the entire blockchain network. If a malicious actor gains control of the network, they can alter or delete transaction records, compromise data privacy, and cause confusion and chaos in the system. This can lead to a loss of trust in the blockchain network, which can be difficult to regain.

In addition to 51% attacks, there are other network consensus issues that can pose a security risk to blockchain networks. One of these is the Sybil attack, which occurs when an attacker creates multiple fake identities on a network to gain control of the network's resources. This allows the attacker to manipulate the network's consensus mechanism and potentially compromise the integrity of the blockchain.

To mitigate the risks associated with network consensus issues, blockchain developers are exploring new consensus mechanisms that can offer greater security and scalability. One such mechanism is Proof of Stake (PoS), which relies on validators to secure the network rather than miners. PoS has the potential to be more energy-efficient than Proof of Work (PoW) and could help reduce the risk of 51% attacks.

Overall, the risks associated with network consensus issues are an important consideration for organizations looking to adopt blockchain technology in their supply chain management. To minimize these risks, it is essential to implement robust security measures, stay up-to-date with the latest security best practices, and continually monitor the network for potential threats.

Centralization risks with private blockchains

Blockchain technology has been touted as a decentralized and distributed solution, with no single entity controlling the network or data. However, this is not always the case, particularly with private blockchains. Private blockchains are restricted and controlled by a single organization, or a consortium of organizations, rather than being open to the public.

Centralization risks arise when a single entity controls the majority of nodes in the network, leading to concerns over security, transparency, and trust. In a private blockchain, there is often a lack of transparency as the nodes are controlled by a single entity or consortium, leading to a lack of trust in the network. This creates the risk of collusion and fraud, as the controlling entity or consortium may be able to manipulate the network to their advantage.

In addition, the use of private blockchains can also lead to reduced interoperability with other blockchain networks. This can limit the potential benefits of blockchain technology in supply chain management, as data sharing and collaboration across different networks become more challenging.

To address these centralization risks, it is important to ensure that private blockchains are designed with transparency, security, and openness in mind. The use of independent auditors and regulators can help to ensure that the network is secure and that there is no manipulation or fraud. Additionally, the use of open-source technology can promote transparency and encourage collaboration between different networks.

It is also important to consider the potential benefits and limitations of private blockchains, and to carefully evaluate their suitability for specific use cases. Private blockchains may be more appropriate for use cases where data privacy and confidentiality are critical, such as in the healthcare industry.

Overall, while private blockchains offer several benefits, they also come with significant risks and challenges. Careful consideration and evaluation are necessary to determine whether a private blockchain is appropriate for a particular supply chain management use case, and to ensure that the network is designed with transparency, security, and openness in mind.

Potential for smart contract errors and vulnerabilities

Blockchain technology enables the use of smart contracts that can execute self-executing agreements, automate business processes, and enable decentralized applications. Smart contracts are code stored on a blockchain that automatically execute the terms of an agreement when certain conditions are met. While smart contracts provide numerous benefits, they also present some security challenges that must be addressed.

One major challenge associated with smart contracts is the potential for errors and vulnerabilities in the code. If the code contains a flaw, it can be exploited by attackers to manipulate the terms of the contract and steal funds or assets. Smart contract errors can occur due to a variety of reasons, such as coding errors, incorrect assumptions, or faulty logic.

One notable example of a smart contract vulnerability is the DAO (Decentralized Autonomous Organization) hack in 2016. The DAO was a venture capital fund that operated on the Ethereum blockchain and was governed by a smart contract. In June 2016, an attacker exploited a vulnerability in the code of the DAO smart contract, allowing them to siphon off millions of dollars worth of Ether, the cryptocurrency used on the Ethereum blockchain.

The DAO hack highlighted the importance of auditing smart contract code to identify potential vulnerabilities. Smart contract auditing involves reviewing the code to ensure that it is secure and functions as intended. Auditors use tools such as formal verification, which is a mathematical method of verifying the correctness of a program, and manual code review to identify potential security issues.

In addition to errors and vulnerabilities in smart contract code, there are also risks associated with the execution of smart contracts. Once a smart contract is deployed on a blockchain, it cannot be changed, and the code is executed automatically based on predefined rules. If these rules are not carefully designed, they can lead to unintended consequences, such as the loss of funds or assets.

For example, in 2017, a smart contract called Parity was deployed on the Ethereum blockchain. The contract contained a bug that allowed anyone to take control of the contract and freeze the funds held within it. As a result, over $300 million worth of Ether was frozen, and the funds remain inaccessible to this day.

To mitigate the risks associated with smart contracts, it is important to design them carefully, audit the code thoroughly, and test them extensively before deployment. In addition, blockchain developers and organizations must also consider the potential legal and regulatory implications of smart contracts, particularly in industries such as finance and insurance, where contracts must comply with complex regulations.

Another important consideration when using smart contracts is the potential for unintended consequences. Smart contracts are designed to execute automatically, based on predefined rules encoded in the code. However, these rules may not always be appropriate for every situation. For example, if a smart contract is designed to automatically execute a trade when certain conditions are met, but those conditions are no longer relevant, the contract may still execute the trade, resulting in unintended consequences.

To address this issue, blockchain developers and organizations must carefully consider the design of their smart contracts and ensure that they are flexible enough to adapt to changing circumstances. They must also develop clear guidelines for when and how smart contracts can be modified or terminated, to prevent unintended consequences and ensure compliance with legal and regulatory requirements.

In conclusion, while smart contracts offer numerous benefits, they also present significant security challenges that must be addressed. These challenges include the potential for errors and vulnerabilities in the code, risks associated with the execution of smart contracts, and legal and regulatory implications. To mitigate these risks, blockchain developers and organizations must carefully design, audit, and test their smart contracts, and ensure that they are flexible enough to adapt to changing circumstances.

Chapter 3: Organizational Challenges
Resistance to change and lack of buy-in from stakeholders

Blockchain technology has the potential to revolutionize many industries, including supply chain management, by increasing transparency, reducing fraud, and improving efficiency. However, implementing blockchain technology is not without its challenges. One of the most significant obstacles is resistance to change and lack of buy-in from stakeholders. In this chapter, we will explore this challenge and examine some strategies to overcome it.

Resistance to change is a common obstacle in any organizational change initiative, and implementing blockchain technology is no exception. Some stakeholders may view blockchain as a threat to their established ways of working, while others may simply be skeptical of new technology. Therefore, it is essential to understand why stakeholders may resist the implementation of blockchain technology and how to address their concerns.

One of the main reasons stakeholders resist change is fear of the unknown. They may feel that the new technology is untested and could introduce risks to the organization. It is essential to provide stakeholders with a clear understanding of the technology and its benefits, as well as any potential risks or challenges. This can be done through workshops, training, and educational materials that explain the technology in plain language.

Another reason for resistance to change is a lack of understanding of how the technology will affect their work. Blockchain technology has the potential to disrupt established workflows and processes, and some stakeholders may be concerned about how they will need to adapt to these changes. It is essential to involve stakeholders in the design and implementation process and provide them with a clear understanding of how the technology will affect their work.

Resistance to change can also be due to a lack of trust in the technology or the organization implementing it. This can be addressed by building trust through transparency and accountability. For example, involving stakeholders in the design and implementation process and providing them with regular updates on progress can help build trust.

Finally, resistance to change can be due to a lack of incentives. Stakeholders may not see the benefit of implementing blockchain technology or may not have a personal stake in its success. Therefore, it is essential to provide incentives that align with stakeholders' interests, such as cost savings or improved efficiency.

To overcome resistance to change, it is essential to create a comprehensive change management plan that addresses the concerns of stakeholders. This plan should include communication and training strategies, involve stakeholders in the design and implementation process, build trust through transparency and accountability, and provide incentives that align with stakeholders' interests.

In conclusion, resistance to change and lack of buy-in from stakeholders is a significant challenge when implementing blockchain technology in supply chain management. To overcome this challenge, it is essential to understand the reasons behind stakeholders' resistance and address their concerns through education, involvement, transparency, and incentives. By doing so, organizations can increase the chances of a successful implementation and reap the benefits of blockchain technology in supply chain management.

Limited functionality of blockchain technology in supply chain management

Blockchain technology has been touted as a revolutionary tool for supply chain management, but it also has its limitations. In this section, we'll explore the limitations of blockchain technology in supply chain management.

One of the most significant limitations of blockchain technology in supply chain management is its limited functionality. While blockchain technology offers several benefits, such as transparency, security, and traceability, it's not a cure-all solution for every supply chain issue.

One of the biggest limitations is that blockchain technology cannot capture all the data that is necessary for managing complex supply chains. For example, blockchain technology is not well suited for capturing data about the physical characteristics of a product, such as temperature, humidity, or pressure. This is because blockchain technology relies on digital data that can be easily recorded and transferred between parties. Physical data, on the other hand, requires sensors and other technologies that can be expensive and difficult to implement.

Another limitation of blockchain technology is its inability to capture and process unstructured data. Unstructured data includes data that is not organized in a predefined manner, such as social media posts or customer feedback. While blockchain technology can be used to capture structured data, such as purchase orders or invoices, it struggles to capture and analyze unstructured data.

In addition to its limited functionality, blockchain technology can also be challenging to integrate into existing supply chain systems. This is because many organizations have invested heavily in their current systems and may be hesitant to adopt new technologies that require significant changes to their current processes. This can lead to resistance to change and slow adoption rates, which can limit the effectiveness of blockchain technology in supply chain management.

Another challenge with implementing blockchain technology in supply chain management is the need for collaboration among stakeholders. Implementing blockchain technology requires the participation and cooperation of all parties involved in the supply chain, including suppliers, manufacturers, distributors, and customers. Achieving this level of collaboration can be challenging, especially if there is a lack of trust or transparency among stakeholders.

Finally, the cost of implementing blockchain technology in supply chain management can be significant. While the cost of implementing blockchain technology has decreased over the years, it can still be prohibitively expensive for some organizations. This can make it difficult for smaller organizations to adopt blockchain technology, which can limit its impact on the supply chain as a whole.

In conclusion, while blockchain technology offers several benefits for supply chain management, it also has its limitations. Blockchain technology's limited functionality, difficulty integrating with existing systems, and need for collaboration among stakeholders can all limit its effectiveness in supply chain management. Additionally, the cost of implementing blockchain technology can be a significant barrier for some organizations. As such, organizations should carefully consider these limitations when deciding whether or not to adopt blockchain technology in their supply chain management systems.

Limited standardization and fragmentation of blockchain networks

One of the key challenges facing the adoption of blockchain technology in supply chain management is the lack of standardization and fragmentation of blockchain networks. While blockchain technology offers many benefits for supply chain management, the lack of a common framework and standardization can make it difficult for organizations to effectively integrate blockchain into their supply chain processes.

1. Standardization challenges in blockchain networks

One of the key challenges with blockchain networks is the lack of standardization. There is no one-size-fits-all solution for blockchain implementation, which makes it difficult for organizations to adopt blockchain technology. Different blockchain networks have different protocols, consensus mechanisms, and data storage requirements, which can make it difficult to transfer data between different networks. This lack of standardization also makes it difficult for organizations to choose the right blockchain network for their specific needs.

Another challenge with standardization in blockchain networks is the lack of consensus among different organizations. Blockchain networks are decentralized, which means that there is no central authority to make decisions on behalf of the network. Instead, decisions are made by the network participants through consensus mechanisms. However, achieving consensus among different organizations can be challenging, especially when there are competing interests and incentives.

2. Fragmentation challenges in blockchain networks

Another challenge facing the adoption of blockchain technology in supply chain management is the fragmentation of blockchain networks. Fragmentation refers to the existence of multiple blockchain networks, each with their own protocols, standards, and data storage requirements. This fragmentation can make it difficult for organizations to exchange data between different networks, which can limit the effectiveness of blockchain technology in supply chain management.

Fragmentation can also make it difficult for organizations to choose the right blockchain network for their specific needs. With so many different blockchain networks available, it can be difficult to determine which network is the most appropriate for a particular application.

3. Implications for supply chain management

The lack of standardization and fragmentation in blockchain networks can have several implications for supply chain management. First, it can limit the effectiveness of blockchain technology in supply chain management. Without a common framework and standardization, it can be difficult for organizations to effectively integrate blockchain into their supply chain processes.

Second, it can create additional costs for organizations. The lack of standardization and fragmentation can make it difficult for organizations to choose the right blockchain network for their specific needs, which can lead to additional costs associated with implementation and maintenance.

Finally, it can limit the scalability of blockchain technology in supply chain management. Without standardization and fragmentation, it can be difficult to scale blockchain networks to meet the needs of large organizations with complex supply chains.

4. Addressing standardization and fragmentation challenges

To address the standardization and fragmentation challenges facing blockchain networks, several initiatives have been launched to develop common frameworks and standards. For example, the International Organization for Standardization (ISO) has developed several standards for blockchain technology, including ISO 22739:2017, which provides guidelines for the use of blockchain in supply chain management.

Other initiatives, such as the Enterprise Ethereum Alliance (EEA) and the Hyperledger Project, are working to develop open-source blockchain frameworks that can be used across different industries and applications. These initiatives aim to provide a common framework and standardization for blockchain networks, which can help to overcome the challenges of fragmentation and standardization.

Additionally, consortiums and partnerships between organizations can help to overcome fragmentation challenges by promoting interoperability between different blockchain networks. These partnerships can help to develop common protocols and standards for blockchain networks, which can help to promote greater interoperability and exchange of data between different networks.

Difficulty of implementation and need for specialized expertise

While blockchain technology has the potential to revolutionize supply chain management, its implementation is not without its challenges. One of the most significant hurdles faced by organizations seeking to adopt blockchain technology is the difficulty of implementation and the need for specialized expertise.

Implementation Challenges

The implementation of blockchain technology can be a complex and costly process. Organizations need to assess their existing systems and determine how blockchain can be integrated into their operations. This requires an understanding of the different blockchain platforms and their capabilities, as well as an understanding of the specific requirements of the supply chain management process.

In addition to the technical challenges of implementation, organizations must also consider the impact on their existing processes and the need for new policies and procedures. They must also assess the costs and benefits of implementing blockchain technology, including the potential return on investment (ROI) and the cost of maintaining and upgrading the technology.

Specialized Expertise

Another significant challenge faced by organizations seeking to adopt blockchain technology is the need for specialized expertise. Blockchain technology is complex, and its implementation requires specialized skills and knowledge. This includes an understanding of the different blockchain platforms and their capabilities, as well as an understanding of programming languages such as Solidity.

Furthermore, the development and deployment of smart contracts require specialized skills and knowledge. Organizations may need to hire or train specialized personnel to develop and manage blockchain systems, which can be costly and time-consuming.

In addition, the lack of standardized processes and technologies for implementing blockchain technology can also present challenges. The variety of platforms, protocols, and technologies used in different blockchain implementations can make it difficult to find qualified experts with experience in specific areas.

Solutions and Best Practices

To address the challenges of implementing blockchain technology in supply chain management, organizations can take several steps:

1. Conduct a thorough assessment of their existing systems and determine how blockchain technology can be integrated into their operations.

2. Hire or train specialized personnel with expertise in blockchain technology, programming languages, and smart contract development.

3. Work with vendors and partners who have experience in implementing blockchain technology in supply chain management.

4. Participate in industry groups and consortia to share knowledge and best practices and to collaborate on the development of standards for blockchain technology.

5. Implement a pilot program to test the technology before rolling it out across the organization.

6. Develop policies and procedures to ensure the security and integrity of the blockchain network.

Conclusion

While the adoption of blockchain technology in supply chain management is not without its challenges, the benefits of using blockchain technology can far outweigh the costs. Organizations must carefully consider the technical, organizational, and security challenges of implementation and take steps to address them.

By conducting a thorough assessment of their existing systems, hiring or training specialized personnel, working with experienced vendors and partners, participating in industry groups and consortia, implementing pilot programs, and developing policies and procedures, organizations can successfully implement blockchain technology and reap the benefits of increased transparency, efficiency, and security in their supply chain management processes.

Challenges in managing and maintaining decentralized networks

Decentralized networks, such as those used in blockchain technology, are characterized by their distributed nature, where multiple nodes or devices are connected to form a network. The management and maintenance of such networks can present a number of challenges for organizations, particularly in the context of supply chain management.

1. Governance and decision-making

One of the key challenges in managing decentralized networks is governance and decision-making. Unlike centralized networks, where a single entity or group is responsible for making decisions and managing the network, decentralized networks rely on a consensus mechanism to make decisions. This can make it difficult for organizations to establish clear lines of responsibility and accountability for network governance.

In the context of supply chain management, this can be particularly challenging. Supply chains involve multiple parties, including suppliers, manufacturers, distributors, and retailers, each with their own interests and priorities. This can make it difficult to achieve consensus on network governance, particularly in cases where different parties have competing interests.

To address this challenge, organizations may need to develop governance structures that facilitate collaboration and consensus-building. This could involve the establishment of formal committees or working groups to oversee network governance, or the development of clear protocols for decision-making and conflict resolution.

2. Network maintenance and security

Another key challenge in managing decentralized networks is network maintenance and security. Decentralized networks are vulnerable to a range of security threats, including hacking, data breaches, and denial-of-service attacks. In addition, the maintenance of decentralized networks requires ongoing monitoring and maintenance to ensure that the network is functioning properly.

In the context of supply chain management, this can be particularly challenging, as supply chains involve multiple parties with varying levels of technical expertise and resources. This can make it difficult to ensure that all parties are adhering to the necessary security protocols and that the network is being adequately monitored and maintained.

To address this challenge, organizations may need to develop clear protocols for network maintenance and security. This could involve the development of formal policies and procedures for network monitoring and maintenance, as well as the establishment of training and education programs to ensure that all parties are aware of their responsibilities and are equipped with the necessary skills and resources.

3. Scalability and interoperability

A third challenge in managing decentralized networks is scalability and interoperability. Decentralized networks are often characterized by their limited scalability, as the addition of new nodes or devices can result in increased network latency and reduced network performance. In addition, the lack of interoperability between different blockchain networks can make it difficult for organizations to integrate and manage multiple networks.

In the context of supply chain management, this can be particularly challenging, as supply chains involve multiple parties with varying levels of technical expertise and resources. This can make it difficult to ensure that all parties are adhering to the necessary protocols and that the network is functioning properly.

To address this challenge, organizations may need to invest in technologies and tools that can help to improve network scalability and interoperability. This could involve the development of new blockchain protocols that are specifically designed for supply chain management, as well as the integration of existing blockchain networks with other technologies such as the Internet of Things (IoT) and artificial intelligence (AI).

4. Cost and resource allocation

Managing and maintaining a decentralized network can be costly and resource-intensive. Unlike centralized systems where maintenance is handled by a single entity, decentralized networks require continuous monitoring and maintenance by a network of participants. This can be a significant challenge, particularly for smaller organizations with limited resources.

One of the main costs associated with managing and maintaining a decentralized network is the cost of computing power. Decentralized networks rely on a distributed network of nodes to verify transactions and maintain the integrity of the network. Each node requires a significant amount of computing power, which can be expensive to maintain.

Another cost associated with managing and maintaining a decentralized network is the cost of storage. Decentralized networks require a significant amount of storage capacity to store the blockchain ledger and associated data. The cost of storage can be significant, particularly for larger networks.

In addition to computing power and storage costs, there are other costs associated with managing and maintaining a decentralized network. These include the cost of network infrastructure, such as servers and networking equipment, as well as the cost of security measures such as firewalls and encryption.

Resource allocation is another challenge associated with managing and maintaining a decentralized network. Because decentralized networks rely on a network of participants to verify transactions and maintain the network, it can be difficult to allocate resources effectively. In some cases, network participants may be unwilling or unable to allocate the necessary resources to maintain the network, which can lead to security and performance issues.

To address these challenges, organizations may need to consider strategies such as incentivizing network participants to contribute computing power and storage capacity, as well as investing in infrastructure and security measures to ensure the stability and security of the network. Additionally, organizations may need to consider partnering with other organizations to share the costs and resources associated with maintaining a decentralized network.

5. Regulatory challenges

Decentralized networks can also face significant regulatory challenges. Because decentralized networks operate outside of traditional regulatory frameworks, they can be subject to a complex and evolving regulatory landscape.

One of the main regulatory challenges facing decentralized networks is the lack of clarity around how existing regulations apply to blockchain technology. For example, regulations around data privacy and protection may need to be adapted to account for the unique characteristics of blockchain networks. Additionally, regulations around anti-money laundering (AML) and know-your-customer (KYC) compliance may need to be adapted to account for the decentralized nature of blockchain transactions.

Another regulatory challenge facing decentralized networks is the lack of global regulatory standards. Because blockchain technology is still relatively new, there is a lack of consensus around regulatory standards, which can create uncertainty for organizations operating in multiple jurisdictions.

Finally, there is the risk of regulatory arbitrage, where organizations may choose to operate in jurisdictions with more favorable regulatory environments, leading to a lack of consistency in how blockchain networks are regulated around the world.

To address these challenges, organizations may need to work closely with regulators to ensure that their blockchain networks are compliant with existing regulations, while also advocating for the development of clear and consistent global regulatory standards for blockchain technology. Additionally, organizations may need to consider developing their own internal compliance programs to ensure that they are meeting regulatory requirements in all jurisdictions where they operate.

Ethical and social implications of blockchain technology

While blockchain technology offers several benefits for organizations, including increased transparency, efficiency, and security, there are also several ethical and social implications that must be considered. These implications arise from the fact that blockchain is a decentralized technology that can potentially disrupt existing power structures and redistribute power to new entities. This section explores some of the ethical and social implications of blockchain technology.

1. Disintermediation and the role of intermediaries

One of the most significant ethical and social implications of blockchain technology is disintermediation, which refers to the removal of intermediaries such as banks, governments, and other third-party entities from transactions. While disintermediation can potentially increase efficiency and reduce costs, it can also have negative consequences, such as the loss of jobs and the concentration of power in the hands of a few entities. For example, the widespread adoption of blockchain technology in the financial sector could lead to the displacement of traditional banks and financial institutions, which could have negative consequences for their employees and the wider economy.

2. Decentralization and power structures

Blockchain technology is based on decentralization, which means that it is not controlled by any single entity or organization. This has the potential to disrupt existing power structures and redistribute power to new entities. However, it is important to consider who these new entities are and whether they are accountable to the wider society. For example, if a new blockchain-based platform emerges that dominates a particular sector, it could have significant power over the industry and potentially abuse this power. It is important to ensure that there are mechanisms in place to hold such entities accountable.

3. Privacy and data protection

Blockchain technology is often associated with transparency and immutability, but it also raises concerns about privacy and data protection. For example, while blockchain-based platforms can be used to store and share personal data securely and efficiently, there is also the risk that this data could be accessed by unauthorized parties. It is important to ensure that appropriate measures are in place to protect personal data on blockchain-based platforms.

4. Digital identity and inclusion

Blockchain technology has the potential to enable new forms of digital identity and inclusion. For example, blockchain-based digital identities could provide a secure and decentralized way for individuals to prove their identity and access services. However, there are also concerns that the use of blockchain technology could exacerbate existing inequalities, particularly if certain groups are excluded from accessing blockchain-based services.

5. Environmental impact

The increasing popularity of blockchain technology has also raised concerns about its environmental impact. The energy-intensive nature of blockchain-based mining and verification processes has led to criticism that the technology is unsustainable and contributes to climate change. It is important to consider the environmental impact of blockchain technology and explore ways to reduce its carbon footprint.

Overall, while blockchain technology offers several benefits for organizations, it also raises several ethical and social implications that must be considered. Organizations must carefully weigh the benefits and risks of blockchain adoption and ensure that appropriate measures are in place to mitigate the negative consequences. It is important to work collaboratively to develop ethical and socially responsible uses of blockchain technology that benefit society as a whole.

Chapter 4: Financial Challenges
High cost of implementing and maintaining blockchain technology

Introduction Blockchain technology has gained increasing attention in recent years due to its potential to revolutionize the way organizations conduct financial transactions. However, the implementation of blockchain technology comes with significant financial challenges. In this section, we will discuss the high costs associated with implementing and maintaining blockchain technology in supply chain management.

High Cost of Implementation One of the major challenges organizations face when implementing blockchain technology is the high cost involved. Implementing a blockchain-based system requires significant investment in hardware, software, and human resources. Moreover, the cost of acquiring blockchain technology can be high due to the limited number of vendors in the market.

Organizations need to invest in specialized hardware to support the decentralized architecture of blockchain technology. This hardware is expensive and requires regular maintenance and upgrades to ensure optimal performance. Additionally, organizations must invest in specialized software to develop and deploy blockchain-based applications.

The cost of human resources is another significant challenge organizations face when implementing blockchain technology. The complexity of blockchain technology requires specialized skills that are scarce in the market. Organizations must invest in training and hiring personnel with the necessary skills to develop, deploy, and maintain blockchain-based applications.

High Cost of Maintenance Maintaining a blockchain-based system can be expensive. The decentralized architecture of blockchain technology requires a significant amount of computing power and energy to ensure the network's stability and security. Organizations must invest in the necessary infrastructure to support the network's computing power, which can be expensive.

Moreover, maintaining a blockchain-based system requires constant monitoring and updating to ensure optimal performance and security. The decentralized nature of blockchain technology means that any issues that arise must be addressed immediately to prevent them from spreading and affecting the entire network. This requires a dedicated team of experts who are available 24/7 to monitor the system and address any issues that arise.

Cost and Resource Allocation The high cost of implementing and maintaining blockchain technology means that organizations must carefully allocate their resources. This requires a careful analysis of the organization's financial position, budget constraints, and long-term strategic objectives.

Organizations must consider the opportunity cost of investing in blockchain technology. They must weigh the potential benefits of implementing blockchain technology against the cost of doing so. In some cases, the cost of implementing blockchain technology may outweigh the potential benefits, making it unfeasible for organizations to pursue.

Moreover, organizations must consider the cost of allocating resources to maintain a blockchain-based system. This includes the cost of hiring specialized personnel, investing in infrastructure, and conducting regular maintenance and updates. Organizations must ensure that they have the necessary resources to maintain the system for the long term.

Conclusion Implementing blockchain technology in supply chain management comes with significant financial challenges. The high cost of implementation and maintenance requires organizations to carefully allocate their resources and weigh the potential benefits against the cost of doing so. Organizations must ensure that they have the necessary resources to maintain the system for the long term to reap the benefits of blockchain technology.

Limited return on investment for some organizations

One of the main financial challenges that organizations face when adopting blockchain technology in supply chain management is the limited return on investment (ROI) that they may experience. While blockchain technology can potentially provide significant benefits such as increased efficiency, transparency, and security, the costs associated with implementing and maintaining the technology may outweigh these benefits for some organizations.

One of the main reasons for the limited ROI of blockchain technology is the high cost of implementation and maintenance. As discussed earlier, implementing blockchain technology requires significant investment in terms of both financial resources and time. This investment can be especially daunting for small and medium-sized enterprises (SMEs), which may not have the financial resources to make such a significant investment.

In addition to the high cost of implementation and maintenance, organizations may also experience limited ROI due to the limited scalability and interoperability of blockchain networks. As discussed earlier, blockchain networks may not be able to handle the volume of transactions required for large-scale supply chains, and may not be compatible with existing legacy systems. This can limit the potential benefits of blockchain technology for organizations, and may lead to a lower ROI than initially anticipated.

Another factor that can contribute to limited ROI is the lack of standardization in the blockchain industry. As discussed earlier, there are currently multiple blockchain platforms and protocols available, each with their own unique features and capabilities. This can make it difficult for organizations to choose the right platform and protocol for their specific supply chain needs, and may lead to a lower ROI if they choose the wrong platform.

Furthermore, the lack of regulatory frameworks and legal frameworks for blockchain technology can also contribute to limited ROI. Without clear regulations and legal frameworks in place, organizations may be hesitant to adopt blockchain technology due to concerns about legal and regulatory compliance. This can limit the potential benefits of blockchain technology for organizations and lead to a lower ROI.

To address these challenges and increase the ROI of blockchain technology, organizations can take several steps. One approach is to carefully evaluate the costs and benefits of implementing blockchain technology and develop a clear strategy for implementation. This can involve conducting a cost-benefit analysis to determine whether the benefits of blockchain technology outweigh the costs, and developing a clear plan for implementation and maintenance.

Organizations can also explore different funding options for blockchain technology, such as government grants or venture capital investments. This can help to alleviate some of the financial burden of implementing blockchain technology and increase the potential ROI.

In addition, organizations can work to address the challenges of scalability, interoperability, and standardization by collaborating with other organizations and industry partners. By working together to develop common standards and protocols for blockchain technology, organizations can increase the potential benefits of blockchain technology and improve the ROI.

Overall, while the limited ROI of blockchain technology may be a concern for some organizations, there are steps that can be taken to address these challenges and increase the potential benefits of the technology. By carefully evaluating the costs and benefits of implementation, exploring different funding options, and collaborating with industry partners, organizations can maximize the ROI of blockchain technology in supply chain management.

Challenges associated with pricing and revenue models

Blockchain technology has the potential to significantly transform traditional business models and value chains. However, its unique characteristics and infrastructure also present significant challenges when it comes to pricing and revenue models. This section will explore some of the key challenges associated with pricing and revenue models for blockchain-based applications.

1. Difficulty in pricing decentralized systems

One of the primary challenges associated with pricing blockchain-based systems is the lack of a clear pricing model. This is because blockchain networks are often decentralized, and users contribute to the network's operations in various ways, making it difficult to assign a value to each user's contribution.

Traditional pricing models such as pay-per-use, subscription-based, or licensing fees may not be appropriate for blockchain-based applications. These models are designed for centralized systems where there is a clear owner or operator responsible for providing the service. In a decentralized blockchain network, there is no central authority, and users can access the network's services directly.

The lack of a clear pricing model can make it difficult for blockchain-based applications to generate revenue, as users may be reluctant to pay for services without a clear understanding of their value.

2. Revenue sharing and incentive models

In addition to pricing challenges, blockchain networks also present challenges when it comes to revenue sharing and incentive models. Since blockchain networks are decentralized, there is no central authority responsible for distributing revenue or incentives.

Instead, revenue sharing and incentive models must be built into the blockchain network's code. This presents challenges for developers who must balance the need to incentivize users to contribute to the network's operations while also ensuring that the network remains secure and efficient.

One approach to revenue sharing is to use a token or cryptocurrency as the network's native currency. Users can earn tokens by contributing to the network's operations, and these tokens can then be used to access the network's services or traded on a cryptocurrency exchange.

However, this approach also presents challenges, as the value of cryptocurrencies can be highly volatile, making it difficult to assign a stable value to network contributions. Additionally, cryptocurrency exchanges can be subject to fraud, hacks, and other security vulnerabilities, which can put users' investments at risk.

3. Limited monetization opportunities

Another challenge associated with blockchain-based applications is limited monetization opportunities. In many cases, blockchain networks are designed to provide a public good, such as secure and transparent record-keeping, rather than to generate revenue.

For example, blockchain networks used for supply chain management may be designed to increase transparency and traceability, rather than to generate revenue. While these networks may provide value to businesses and consumers, they may not generate direct revenue for the network's operators.

This can make it difficult for organizations to justify the cost of developing and maintaining a blockchain-based application. In some cases, organizations may need to explore alternative revenue streams, such as advertising or data analytics, to offset the costs associated with blockchain development.

4. Competition from centralized alternatives

Finally, blockchain-based applications also face competition from traditional, centralized alternatives. While blockchain technology has the potential to transform industries, many organizations may be hesitant to adopt blockchain-based solutions due to the perceived risk and uncertainty associated with a decentralized infrastructure.

For example, a traditional cloud-based database may be perceived as a safer and more reliable option than a decentralized blockchain network. While blockchain technology may offer additional benefits such as increased transparency and security, organizations may prioritize familiarity and reliability over potential benefits.

This can make it difficult for blockchain-based applications to compete with traditional alternatives, as they may struggle to attract users and generate revenue.

In conclusion, pricing and revenue models are essential for the success of any business model, including blockchain-based applications. However, the decentralized and complex nature of blockchain networks presents unique challenges when it comes to

Difficulty in measuring and proving ROI

The potential return on investment (ROI) for implementing blockchain technology has been a topic of discussion since the technology's inception. While many companies have reported success in using blockchain to streamline processes, increase efficiency, and reduce costs, measuring the actual ROI of these initiatives can be difficult. In this section, we will explore the challenges associated with measuring and proving ROI for blockchain implementations.

1. Lack of Established Metrics One of the primary challenges of measuring blockchain ROI is the lack of established metrics. Traditional ROI metrics such as payback period, net present value, and internal rate of return may not be sufficient for evaluating blockchain implementations. This is because blockchain technology is often used for process improvements rather than direct revenue generation, and the benefits of these improvements may not be easily quantifiable.

2. Difficulty in Data Collection Another challenge of measuring blockchain ROI is the difficulty in collecting data. Blockchain implementations often involve multiple parties, and it can be challenging to obtain accurate data from all parties involved. Additionally, the data stored on the blockchain is often highly encrypted and anonymized, which can make it difficult to extract useful insights.

3. Limited Industry Benchmarks Another challenge of measuring blockchain ROI is the limited industry benchmarks. With blockchain technology still being relatively new, there are few established benchmarks for measuring ROI in specific industries. This can make it challenging for companies to compare their blockchain initiatives with industry standards and assess their performance.

4. Complexity of Blockchain Implementations The complexity of blockchain implementations can also make it challenging to measure ROI. Blockchain implementations often require significant investment in infrastructure, software

development, and ongoing maintenance. These costs can be difficult to accurately calculate, and the benefits of the implementation may not be fully realized for several years.

5. Lack of Long-Term Data Finally, the lack of long-term data can make it difficult to measure the ROI of blockchain implementations. Many blockchain initiatives are relatively new and have not yet been fully tested over an extended period. This can make it challenging to accurately assess the long-term benefits and costs of the implementation.

Despite these challenges, it is essential to attempt to measure the ROI of blockchain implementations. This can help companies identify areas where improvements can be made, and it can provide valuable data for future blockchain initiatives. Some strategies that companies can use to measure and prove ROI include developing custom metrics, conducting comprehensive data analysis, and collaborating with industry partners to establish benchmarks.

In conclusion, measuring and proving ROI for blockchain implementations can be challenging due to the lack of established metrics, difficulty in data collection, limited industry benchmarks, complexity of implementations, and lack of long-term data. However, companies should still attempt to measure the ROI of their blockchain initiatives, as this can provide valuable insights and identify areas for improvement. By developing custom metrics, conducting comprehensive data analysis, and collaborating with industry partners, companies can overcome some of the challenges associated with measuring blockchain ROI.

Challenges in securing funding for blockchain projects

One of the significant challenges facing blockchain projects is securing adequate funding. Developing a blockchain project requires significant investment, which can be challenging to obtain, particularly in the early stages. Despite the growing interest in blockchain technology, many investors and financial institutions remain cautious about investing in blockchain projects due to the technology's perceived risks and uncertainties. In this section, we discuss the challenges facing blockchain projects in securing funding and the possible solutions.

1. Lack of awareness and understanding

One of the primary reasons why blockchain projects struggle to secure funding is the lack of awareness and understanding of the technology's potential benefits. Many investors and financial institutions are still unfamiliar with the workings of blockchain technology and its potential applications. As a result, they may be hesitant to invest in a technology that they do not fully understand. The lack of awareness and understanding of blockchain technology can also make it challenging to evaluate the potential risks and rewards of investing in blockchain projects.

2. Regulatory uncertainty

Another significant challenge facing blockchain projects in securing funding is regulatory uncertainty. The regulatory landscape surrounding blockchain technology is still evolving, and different countries and jurisdictions have different regulations concerning blockchain technology. The lack of clarity and consistency in the regulatory framework for blockchain projects can make it difficult for investors to assess the regulatory risks associated with investing in such projects.

3. Lack of scalability

Scalability is another challenge facing blockchain projects in securing funding. Many blockchain projects are still in the early stages of development and have yet to demonstrate their scalability. The lack of scalability can make it challenging to attract investors, particularly institutional investors, who require projects to have a clear path to scalability and sustainability.

4. Volatility and liquidity

The volatility and liquidity of cryptocurrencies and other blockchain assets can also make it challenging to secure funding for blockchain projects. The value of cryptocurrencies and other blockchain assets can be highly volatile, making it difficult to determine their true value. The lack of liquidity in many blockchain assets can also make it challenging to convert these assets into fiat currency, which is necessary for many investors and financial institutions.

5. Solutions for securing funding

Despite the challenges facing blockchain projects in securing funding, there are several solutions that blockchain projects can adopt to address these challenges. One solution is to improve awareness and understanding of blockchain technology among investors and financial institutions. Blockchain projects can achieve this by engaging in education and outreach programs aimed at improving awareness and understanding of blockchain technology.

Another solution is to address regulatory uncertainty by working with regulators to develop a regulatory framework that supports blockchain technology. This can involve engaging with policymakers and regulators to provide input on the development of blockchain-related regulations.

Scalability can be addressed by developing and implementing solutions that improve the scalability and sustainability of blockchain projects. These solutions can include the development of new consensus mechanisms, the use of off-chain solutions, and the adoption of new technologies that improve scalability.

Finally, blockchain projects can address the challenges of volatility and liquidity by developing strategies that mitigate these risks. This can involve diversifying the portfolio of blockchain assets, improving liquidity by listing blockchain assets on exchanges, and developing hedging strategies that help to manage the risks associated with volatility and liquidity.

In conclusion, securing funding for blockchain projects can be challenging due to a variety of factors, including lack of awareness and understanding, regulatory uncertainty, scalability, and volatility and liquidity. However, by adopting solutions that improve awareness and understanding, address regulatory uncertainty, improve scalability, and mitigate the risks associated with volatility and liquidity, blockchain projects can increase their chances of securing funding and achieving success.

Challenges in achieving cost efficiencies and scale

One of the promises of blockchain technology is its potential to reduce costs by eliminating intermediaries and streamlining processes. However, achieving cost efficiencies and scale through blockchain implementation is not always straightforward and can be challenging for organizations. In this section, we will explore some of the common challenges in achieving cost efficiencies and scale through blockchain technology.

1. Scalability issues

Scalability is one of the most significant challenges in achieving cost efficiencies and scale through blockchain implementation. Blockchain technology has limitations in terms of the number of transactions it can process per second. For instance, Bitcoin can only handle seven transactions per second, while Ethereum can handle around 15 transactions per second. These limitations make it challenging for blockchain networks to support large-scale applications, such as those required by financial institutions and governments.

To address scalability issues, blockchain developers are exploring various approaches such as sharding, sidechains, and layer-two scaling solutions. Sharding involves splitting the blockchain into smaller parts or shards, with each shard capable of processing a subset of transactions. Sidechains enable the creation of parallel blockchains that can communicate with the main blockchain, reducing the load on the main network. Layer-two scaling solutions, such as payment channels, enable off-chain transactions that do not require every node on the network to process the transaction.

2. Interoperability challenges

Interoperability refers to the ability of different blockchain networks to communicate and transact with each other seamlessly. Achieving interoperability is critical for achieving cost efficiencies and scale through blockchain technology as it enables different networks to work together, reducing redundancies and increasing efficiency. However, achieving interoperability is challenging due to the fragmentation of the blockchain industry, with various blockchain networks using different protocols and standards.

To address interoperability challenges, various initiatives such as the Interledger Protocol (ILP), the Universal Protocol Alliance, and the Blockchain Interoperability Alliance have emerged. These initiatives aim to create standards that enable different blockchain networks to communicate and transact with each other seamlessly.

3. Integration challenges

Integrating blockchain technology into existing systems and processes can be challenging and costly. This is because blockchain networks require significant changes to existing processes and systems to be implemented successfully. For example, to implement a blockchain-based supply chain solution, an organization must reconfigure its existing supply chain processes, integrate the blockchain solution with existing systems such as ERPs, and ensure that all stakeholders are trained on the new processes.

To address integration challenges, blockchain developers are exploring various approaches such as blockchain-as-a-service (BaaS) solutions, which enable organizations to access blockchain infrastructure without incurring the costs and complexities of deploying and managing their own blockchain networks.

4. Regulatory challenges

The regulatory environment surrounding blockchain technology is still developing, and different jurisdictions have varying approaches to regulating blockchain networks. This lack of regulatory clarity can create uncertainty and increase the costs of implementing blockchain technology. For instance, in some jurisdictions, implementing blockchain solutions may require licenses or approvals, which can be time-consuming and costly.

To address regulatory challenges, organizations must ensure that they comply with relevant regulations in their jurisdiction. Additionally, organizations can engage with regulators and industry associations to advocate for clear and consistent regulations for blockchain technology.

5. Security challenges

Implementing blockchain technology can increase security by creating a tamper-proof, decentralized ledger. However, implementing blockchain technology also introduces new security challenges. For example, attackers can exploit vulnerabilities in smart contracts to execute malicious code, and the decentralized nature of blockchain networks can make it challenging to manage and secure the network effectively.

To address security challenges, organizations must adopt a comprehensive security strategy that includes measures such as multi-factor authentication, encryption, and regular security audits. Additionally, organizations can engage with industry associations to develop and promote best

Chapter 5: Legal and Regulatory Challenges
Lack of clear legal framework and regulatory guidance

The lack of a clear legal framework and regulatory guidance is one of the primary challenges facing blockchain technology. Due to the disruptive and innovative nature of blockchain, it is often difficult for legal systems and regulators to keep pace with the technology's rapid developments. As a result, organizations that adopt blockchain may find themselves operating in a legal gray area, with uncertainty around the legality of their activities and potential liabilities.

The lack of regulatory clarity can have significant implications for blockchain technology's adoption and growth. Without a clear legal framework, businesses may be hesitant to invest in blockchain solutions due to the risk of legal repercussions. Additionally, without regulatory guidance, businesses may struggle to navigate complex legal requirements, leading to compliance issues and potential penalties.

One of the primary challenges facing the development of a legal framework for blockchain technology is its decentralized nature. Traditional legal frameworks are designed to regulate centralized organizations and systems, making it difficult to apply them to a decentralized network. As such, new legal frameworks need to be developed that can account for the unique characteristics of blockchain technology.

Another challenge is the lack of international consensus on blockchain regulation. Different countries have taken varying approaches to regulating blockchain technology, with some countries embracing it and others restricting it. The lack of international consensus can create regulatory uncertainty and confusion for organizations that operate across borders.

Additionally, blockchain technology's ability to enable anonymous and pseudonymous transactions has raised concerns about its potential for facilitating criminal activities such as money laundering and terrorism financing. As a result, some governments have been hesitant to fully embrace blockchain technology, fearing it could be used for illicit purposes.

In some cases, governments have attempted to regulate blockchain technology through existing legal frameworks, such as securities regulations. However, applying these frameworks to blockchain technology can be challenging, as the technology's unique features can create ambiguity around whether it qualifies as a security or not.

Another challenge is the lack of clarity around intellectual property rights in the blockchain space. As blockchain technology is open-source and decentralized, it can be challenging to determine who owns the intellectual property associated with specific blockchain applications. This lack of clarity can make it difficult for businesses to invest in blockchain technology, as they may not be able to secure intellectual property rights for their blockchain solutions.

To address these challenges, there is a need for increased collaboration between regulators, policymakers, and the blockchain industry. Regulators need to work closely with the blockchain industry to develop regulatory frameworks that can support innovation while also ensuring compliance with legal requirements. Additionally, the blockchain industry needs to engage with regulators to ensure that their technology is developed in a way that aligns with regulatory requirements.

In conclusion, the lack of a clear legal framework and regulatory guidance is a significant challenge facing blockchain technology. To overcome this challenge, there is a need for increased collaboration between regulators, policymakers, and the blockchain industry to develop regulatory frameworks that can support innovation while also ensuring compliance with legal requirements.

Potential liability and compliance risks

Blockchain technology is transforming various industries by offering greater security, transparency, and accountability. However, with its growing popularity and adoption, it has brought about legal and regulatory challenges. Blockchain technology can pose significant compliance and liability risks for companies that use it for their operations. This chapter discusses the potential liability and compliance risks associated with the use of blockchain technology.

Liability Risks:

Liability risks refer to the legal responsibility that arises from the actions of an individual or organization. Blockchain technology has the potential to increase the liability risks for companies in several ways.

Smart Contracts: Smart contracts are self-executing contracts with the terms of the agreement between buyer and seller being directly written into lines of code. These contracts eliminate the need for intermediaries, and transactions are automatically executed when certain conditions are met. However, smart contracts are not foolproof and can be vulnerable to bugs and errors in the code. If a smart contract malfunctions or contains errors, it can result in financial loss for one or both parties. In such cases, the parties may seek legal action against each other, and the smart contract developer may also face liability for the errors in the code.

Inadequate Security Measures: Blockchain technology offers significant security benefits, but if the security measures are inadequate, it can lead to data breaches and cyber-attacks. If a company's blockchain system is hacked, it can result in data loss, financial loss, and damage to the company's reputation. In such cases, the company may face lawsuits from customers or shareholders who have been affected by the breach.

Fraudulent Transactions: Blockchain technology can be used to facilitate fraudulent activities, such as money laundering, illegal drug sales, and other criminal activities. If a company's blockchain system is used for such activities, it can face legal consequences and reputational damage.

Compliance Risks:

Compliance risks refer to the risks associated with failing to comply with legal and regulatory requirements. Blockchain technology presents several compliance risks for companies.

Data Privacy: Blockchain technology is designed to be transparent and immutable, which means that once data is added to the blockchain, it cannot be altered or deleted. However, this feature can create compliance risks for companies that handle sensitive information. For example, the General Data Protection Regulation (GDPR) in the European Union requires companies to delete personal data upon request by the data subject. If personal data is stored on a blockchain, it cannot be deleted, making it difficult for companies to comply with GDPR requirements.

Anti-Money Laundering (AML) and Know Your Customer (KYC) Regulations: Blockchain technology can be used to facilitate money laundering and other illegal activities. To address this, governments around the world have implemented AML and KYC regulations. Companies that use blockchain technology to facilitate transactions must comply with these regulations, which can be complex and challenging to implement.

Jurisdictional Issues: Blockchain technology is decentralized, which means that it can operate outside of traditional legal and regulatory frameworks. This can create jurisdictional issues, as it may be difficult to determine which laws and regulations apply to a particular blockchain system or transaction. Companies that use blockchain technology must navigate these jurisdictional issues to ensure compliance with applicable laws and regulations.

Blockchain technology presents significant opportunities for companies to improve their operations, increase efficiency, and reduce costs. However, with these opportunities come legal and regulatory challenges that must be addressed. The potential liability and compliance risks associated with the use of blockchain technology require companies to be proactive in implementing adequate security measures and complying with applicable laws and regulations. By doing so, companies can reap the benefits of blockchain technology while minimizing the risks.

Challenges associated with intellectual property and ownership rights

The use of blockchain technology raises important issues related to intellectual property (IP) and ownership rights. Blockchain can be used to create, manage and enforce smart contracts, which can facilitate transactions and agreements without intermediaries. This can disrupt traditional models of IP and ownership rights, particularly in the digital age where assets are often intangible and easily replicated

Background

Intellectual property refers to the legal rights that protect original works of creation, such as inventions, artistic works, and designs. IP laws are designed to encourage innovation and creativity by providing incentives for individuals and companies to invest in research and development, and to create and distribute their works. There are several forms of IP, including patents, trademarks, copyrights, and trade secrets.

Ownership rights refer to the legal rights that individuals and companies have over their property, including their physical and intangible assets. Ownership rights are important for protecting assets and ensuring that individuals and companies can benefit from their investments.

The rise of blockchain technology has created new challenges for IP and ownership rights. Blockchain can be used to create, manage and enforce smart contracts, which can facilitate transactions and agreements without intermediaries. This can disrupt traditional models of IP and ownership rights, particularly in the digital age where assets are often intangible and easily replicated.

Challenges

The use of blockchain technology creates several challenges related to IP and ownership rights. These include:

1. Attribution of ownership: Blockchain technology allows for the creation and management of digital assets, but it can be difficult to attribute ownership to these assets. This is particularly

true for assets that are created collaboratively or that are not clearly defined.

2. Enforcement of IP rights: Smart contracts can be used to enforce IP rights, but it can be difficult to identify and enforce violations. This is particularly true for assets that are created and distributed globally, where different legal systems and jurisdictions may apply.

3. Protection of trade secrets: Blockchain technology can make it difficult to protect trade secrets, as the technology allows for the creation of decentralized, distributed databases. This can make it difficult to prevent unauthorized access and use of trade secrets.

4. Patentability of blockchain technology: There is ongoing debate over whether blockchain technology is patentable, and if so, what aspects of the technology can be patented. This can create uncertainty for companies and individuals who are investing in blockchain technology.

Case study: CryptoKitties

CryptoKitties is a popular blockchain-based game that allows users to collect and breed digital cats. Each CryptoKitty is unique and can be bought, sold, and traded on the Ethereum blockchain. The game has raised several legal and regulatory issues related to IP and ownership rights.

One issue is the ownership of the digital cats. While users can own and trade CryptoKitties on the Ethereum blockchain, it is unclear who owns the underlying intellectual property rights. The creators of the game may own some or all of the IP rights associated with the game, but this has not been confirmed.

Another issue is the potential for infringement of existing IP rights. For example, some CryptoKitties have been created to resemble characters from popular movies and TV shows. This raises questions about whether these CryptoKitties infringe on existing IP rights.

Finally, there is the issue of the patentability of blockchain-based games like CryptoKitties. While there is ongoing debate over whether blockchain technology is patentable, there is little guidance on what aspects of blockchain-based games can be patented.

Regulatory and legal considerations

To address the challenges associated with IP and ownership rights in blockchain technology, regulatory and legal frameworks are needed. These frameworks should provide clear guidance on the ownership, enforcement, and protection of IP rights in blockchain-based assets.

Implications of cross-border transactions and international regulations

Blockchain technology has the potential to revolutionize cross-border transactions by enabling faster, cheaper, and more secure transfers of assets and funds. However, the legal and regulatory landscape surrounding cross-border transactions is complex and highly fragmented. As such, the use of blockchain technology for cross-border transactions is currently facing a number of legal and regulatory challenges.

1. Lack of international regulatory consensus

One of the main challenges facing cross-border blockchain transactions is the lack of international regulatory consensus. The decentralized and borderless nature of blockchain technology presents a significant challenge to regulators, who are struggling to develop a coordinated approach to regulating blockchain-based transactions.

Different countries have different regulatory regimes for blockchain technology, and there is no consensus on how to treat cryptocurrencies, digital assets, and other blockchain-based instruments. This lack of regulatory consistency creates uncertainty and risk for blockchain users and businesses operating across borders.

The lack of regulatory clarity and consensus also presents challenges for compliance and risk management. Companies must navigate a complex web of regulations and compliance requirements in different jurisdictions, which can be time-consuming and costly.

2. Compliance with anti-money laundering and know-your-customer regulations

Cross-border blockchain transactions are also subject to anti-money laundering (AML) and know-your-customer (KYC) regulations. These regulations are designed to prevent the use of blockchain technology for illicit purposes, such as money laundering and terrorism financing.

However, compliance with AML and KYC regulations can be challenging for blockchain users and businesses, especially in cross-border transactions. Different countries have different AML and KYC requirements, and the lack of regulatory consistency makes compliance difficult.

Moreover, the pseudonymous nature of blockchain technology creates challenges for identifying and verifying the identity of users involved in cross-border transactions. This makes it difficult to comply with KYC requirements and detect and prevent money laundering and other illicit activities.

3. Challenges associated with data privacy and protection

Cross-border blockchain transactions involve the transfer of sensitive personal and financial data across borders. This creates challenges for data privacy and protection, as different countries have different data protection laws and regulations.

The General Data Protection Regulation (GDPR) introduced by the European Union imposes strict requirements for the transfer of personal data outside the European Union. Failure to comply with these requirements can result in hefty fines and legal liability.

Moreover, the decentralized and distributed nature of blockchain technology presents additional challenges for data privacy and protection. Personal data stored on a blockchain is accessible to all nodes on the network, which raises concerns about the security and privacy of sensitive information.

4. Cross-border taxation

The use of blockchain technology for cross-border transactions also raises challenges for cross-border taxation. The decentralized and borderless nature of blockchain technology makes it difficult to determine the jurisdiction in which a transaction takes place and the appropriate tax implications.

Different countries have different tax regimes, and there is currently no international consensus on how to tax blockchain-based transactions. The lack of clarity and consistency in cross-border taxation creates uncertainty and risk for blockchain users and businesses operating across borders.

Moreover, the use of cryptocurrencies for cross-border transactions introduces additional challenges for cross-border taxation. Cryptocurrencies are not recognized as legal tender in most countries, and there is currently no consensus on how to tax transactions involving cryptocurrencies.

5. Legal jurisdiction and dispute resolution

Another legal challenge in blockchain technology is determining the appropriate legal jurisdiction and dispute resolution mechanism. Since blockchain networks are decentralized and global, it can be difficult to determine which legal jurisdiction applies to disputes and how they should be resolved.

In traditional business transactions, legal jurisdiction and dispute resolution are typically established through contracts that specify the applicable law and dispute resolution mechanism. However, in the context of blockchain transactions, the lack of a centralized authority and the decentralized nature of the network make it challenging to determine which legal jurisdiction applies in the event of a dispute.

Some blockchain networks have attempted to address this challenge by incorporating dispute resolution mechanisms into their smart contracts. For example, the Ethereum blockchain includes a dispute resolution mechanism called the "Kleros Court," which allows users to resolve disputes through a decentralized arbitration process.

However, these mechanisms are still relatively new and untested, and their effectiveness in resolving disputes remains to be seen. Additionally, there may be challenges in enforcing the decisions of these decentralized arbitration processes in traditional legal systems.

Another approach to addressing legal jurisdiction and dispute resolution challenges in blockchain technology is through the use of private international law. Private international law, also known as conflict of laws, is the body of law that governs legal disputes that involve foreign elements.

Private international law provides rules for determining which legal jurisdiction applies in cross-border disputes and how to resolve them. However, the application of private international law to blockchain disputes may be complicated by the unique characteristics of blockchain technology, such as its decentralized nature and the lack of a centralized authority.

In summary, determining legal jurisdiction and dispute resolution in blockchain transactions is a complex and evolving area of law. While some blockchain networks have attempted to address this challenge through decentralized dispute resolution mechanisms, there is still a need for more guidance and clarity on how to resolve legal disputes in the context of blockchain technology.

Implications of blockchain-based smart contracts on contract law

Blockchain technology has enabled the creation of smart contracts, which are self-executing contracts with the terms of the agreement directly written into code. Smart contracts have the potential to revolutionize contract law by reducing transaction costs, increasing efficiency, and automating contract execution. However, the adoption of smart contracts on blockchain networks raises significant legal and regulatory challenges, particularly in the context of contract law.

One of the key issues associated with blockchain-based smart contracts is the enforceability of the contracts. Traditional contract law is based on the principle of mutual assent, which requires that all parties agree to the terms of the contract before it becomes legally binding. However, smart contracts on blockchain networks are executed automatically, without the need for human intervention, and are designed to operate based on pre-determined rules and conditions. As such, the question arises as to whether the parties to a smart contract have actually agreed to the terms of the contract and whether the contract can be enforced under traditional contract law.

Another issue is the role of intermediaries in the enforcement of smart contracts. In traditional contract law, intermediaries such as lawyers and courts play a crucial role in interpreting and enforcing contracts. However, blockchain-based smart contracts are designed to operate autonomously, without the need for intermediaries. This raises questions about the role of intermediaries in the enforcement of smart contracts and how they can ensure that the terms of the contract are being met.

The use of blockchain-based smart contracts also raises issues related to contract interpretation. Traditional contract law is based on the interpretation of the plain language of the contract, as well as the parties' intent at the time of contracting. However, smart contracts are written in code, which may be difficult for non-technical parties to interpret. This raises questions about how smart contracts can be interpreted and enforced under traditional contract law, particularly if there are disputes about the meaning of the contract.

Furthermore, smart contracts may not always be compatible with existing legal frameworks. For example, smart contracts may not comply with data protection regulations, consumer protection laws, or anti-discrimination laws. This raises questions about how smart contracts can be integrated into existing legal frameworks and how they can be made compatible with existing legal requirements.

Finally, blockchain-based smart contracts may also raise issues related to liability and accountability. Smart contracts are designed to be autonomous and self-executing, which means that they may not be subject to the same level of oversight and accountability as traditional contracts. This raises questions about who is responsible for the actions of smart contracts and how liability can be assigned in the event of a breach or dispute.

To address these challenges, policymakers and legal experts will need to work together to develop new legal frameworks and regulations that are specifically designed for blockchain-based smart contracts. This may involve developing new rules and guidelines for the interpretation and enforcement of smart contracts, as well as establishing new mechanisms for resolving disputes related to smart contracts. It may also require developing new liability frameworks to ensure that parties can be held accountable for the actions of smart contracts.

In conclusion, blockchain-based smart contracts have the potential to revolutionize contract law by increasing efficiency, reducing transaction costs, and automating contract execution. However, the adoption of smart contracts on blockchain networks raises significant legal and regulatory challenges, particularly in the context of contract law. To address these challenges, policymakers and legal experts will need to work together to develop new legal frameworks and regulations that are specifically designed for blockchain-based smart contracts.

Potential for blockchain technology to facilitate illegal activities

One of the major concerns surrounding blockchain technology is the potential for its use in facilitating illegal activities. While blockchain technology has the potential to revolutionize many industries, it also presents new risks that must be addressed. Some of the most significant risks associated with blockchain technology include its use in money laundering, terrorist financing, and other illegal activities.

1. Money laundering and terrorist financing

One of the most significant risks associated with blockchain technology is its potential use in money laundering and terrorist financing. Blockchain technology can be used to anonymously transfer large amounts of funds across borders without the need for intermediaries such as banks. This anonymity makes it difficult for authorities to track and monitor the movement of funds, and could facilitate illegal activities such as money laundering and terrorist financing.

The use of cryptocurrencies, which are often used in conjunction with blockchain technology, has also been linked to illegal activities such as drug trafficking and cybercrime. The decentralized nature of blockchain technology and the lack of regulation in the cryptocurrency market make it an attractive option for criminals looking to launder their funds or finance illegal activities.

2. Illicit markets and activities

Blockchain technology has also been associated with illicit markets and activities, such as the sale of drugs, weapons, and other illegal items on the dark web. Blockchain technology can be used to facilitate these transactions anonymously and securely, making it difficult for authorities to track and identify those involved.

In addition, the use of blockchain technology in voting systems has also raised concerns about the potential for voter fraud and election interference. While blockchain technology has the potential to improve the transparency and security of voting systems, it also presents new risks that must be addressed.

3. Addressing the risks

To address the risks associated with the potential use of blockchain technology in facilitating illegal activities, governments and regulatory bodies must take a proactive approach to regulation and enforcement. This includes developing clear legal frameworks for the use of blockchain technology and cryptocurrencies, as well as implementing effective measures to monitor and regulate their use.

In addition, companies and organizations that are developing blockchain-based solutions must also take steps to ensure that their technologies are not being used for illegal activities. This includes implementing robust anti-money laundering and know-your-customer (KYC) procedures, as well as working closely with law enforcement to identify and address any potential risks.

Finally, it is important for individuals to be aware of the risks associated with blockchain technology and to take steps to protect themselves. This includes being cautious when investing in cryptocurrencies, only using reputable exchanges and wallets, and avoiding engaging in illegal activities that could potentially exploit the anonymity of blockchain technology.

*****

The potential for blockchain technology to facilitate illegal activities is a serious concern that must be addressed by governments, regulatory bodies, and the blockchain industry as a whole. While blockchain technology has the potential to revolutionize many industries, its use in facilitating illegal activities could undermine its potential benefits. By taking a proactive approach to regulation and enforcement, it is possible to mitigate these risks and ensure that blockchain technology is used for the greater good.

Chapter 6: Ethical and Social Challenges
Potential for blockchain technology to exacerbate existing power imbalances

1. Introduction Blockchain technology is often hailed as a solution to many of the world's problems, from reducing fraud to increasing transparency. However, the implementation of blockchain technology can also create new problems and exacerbate existing power imbalances. This chapter will explore the ethical and social challenges associated with blockchain technology, with a focus on the potential for blockchain to exacerbate existing power imbalances.

2. Power Imbalances and Blockchain Technology Power imbalances are a pervasive issue in many industries and societies. They arise when one party or group has more influence, resources, or control than others. Blockchain technology has the potential to exacerbate these power imbalances in several ways.

2.1 Concentration of Power One of the most significant ways in which blockchain technology can exacerbate existing power imbalances is through the concentration of power. Blockchain networks are often designed to reward participants who have the most resources, such as the most powerful computing hardware or the most tokens. As a result, large companies and wealthy individuals have a disproportionate amount of power in blockchain networks, which can further marginalize smaller participants and create new power imbalances.

Moreover, blockchain networks rely on a consensus mechanism to validate transactions and maintain the integrity of the network. In many cases, this consensus mechanism requires a majority or supermajority of participants to agree on a particular course of action. This means that a small group of influential participants could potentially control the entire network, leading to a concentration of power that could be used to benefit their interests at the expense of others.

2.2 Privacy and Security Blockchain technology has the potential to exacerbate power imbalances related to privacy and security. While blockchain networks are often touted as being highly secure and private, the reality is more complex. For example, blockchain transactions are often recorded on a public ledger that anyone can view, which can lead to privacy concerns for individuals or groups that prefer to keep their transactions confidential. Additionally, blockchain networks are vulnerable to hacking and other forms of cyber attacks, which could disproportionately affect smaller participants who lack the resources to protect themselves.

2.3 Environmental Impact The environmental impact of blockchain technology is another area where power imbalances can arise. Blockchain networks are often energy-intensive, requiring significant amounts of electricity to validate transactions and maintain the network. This can create power imbalances related to access to energy and resources, as well as exacerbating existing environmental issues.

3. Ethical Considerations In addition to the social challenges associated with blockchain technology, there are also important ethical considerations to be taken into account.

3.1 Distribution of Benefits One of the most significant ethical considerations associated with blockchain technology is the distribution of benefits. As previously mentioned, blockchain networks are often designed to reward participants who have the most resources, which can further exacerbate existing power imbalances. Moreover, blockchain networks often require significant investments of time, money, and resources to participate effectively, which can be a barrier for smaller organizations or individuals.

This raises important ethical questions about the distribution of benefits and whether blockchain technology is perpetuating existing power imbalances or creating new ones. It is important for stakeholders to consider the potential impact of blockchain technology on different groups and to design networks that are more equitable and accessible.

3.2 Data Privacy and Ownership

Data privacy and ownership is a critical issue that arises with the use of blockchain technology. One of the key features of blockchain technology is the immutability of the data stored on the blockchain, which means that once data is added to the blockchain, it cannot be altered or deleted. While this immutability is a valuable feature for data integrity and security, it can also present challenges for data privacy and ownership.

In traditional systems, data is owned and controlled by centralized entities such as governments, organizations, or individuals. These entities are responsible for ensuring the security and privacy of their data and for complying with data protection regulations. However, in a blockchain system, data is distributed across a decentralized network, and ownership of the data becomes more complex.

One of the main concerns with blockchain technology and data privacy is the potential for personal information to be stored on the blockchain without the knowledge or consent of the individuals involved. This could occur, for example, if an individual's personal data is included in a transaction on the blockchain without their consent. While the data may be encrypted, it is still visible on the blockchain and can potentially be accessed by anyone with access to the network.

Another issue related to data ownership is the potential for conflicts over who owns and controls the data stored on the blockchain. In a decentralized system, it may not be clear who has the right to control or access certain data, particularly if multiple parties are involved in creating or updating the data.

To address these issues, some blockchain systems have implemented mechanisms for data privacy and ownership, such as permissioned blockchains that limit access to certain users or organizations. Other approaches include encrypting data on the blockchain and allowing individuals to control access to their own personal data.

Overall, data privacy and ownership is a complex issue in the context of blockchain technology, and it will require ongoing efforts to develop effective solutions that balance the benefits of blockchain with the need for data privacy and ownership.

3.3 Transparency and Accountability

Another ethical and social challenge associated with blockchain technology is the potential for the technology to exacerbate existing power imbalances and reduce transparency and accountability in decision-making processes.

One of the primary advantages of blockchain technology is its ability to facilitate trust in decentralized systems by providing transparency and accountability. By enabling all network participants to have access to the same information, blockchain technology can reduce the need for intermediaries and increase transparency in decision-making processes.

However, the potential for blockchain technology to reduce transparency and accountability also exists. For example, if certain parties have more resources or computing power than others, they may have greater control over decision-making processes on the blockchain, which could lead to power imbalances.

Additionally, blockchain systems are often complex and difficult to understand, which can make it challenging for users to fully grasp the implications of certain decisions or actions on the network. This lack of transparency can make it difficult for individuals to hold other users or organizations accountable for their actions on the network.

To address these issues, it is important for blockchain systems to prioritize transparency and accountability in their design and implementation. This may include developing user-friendly interfaces and educational resources to help users understand the implications of their actions on the network, as well as implementing governance mechanisms to ensure that all parties have an equal say in decision-making processes.

Overall, while blockchain technology has the potential to increase transparency and accountability in decision-making processes, it also presents challenges that must be addressed to ensure that power imbalances are not exacerbated and that users have access to the information they need to make informed decisions.

3.4 Environmental Impact

Another ethical and social challenge associated with blockchain technology is its environmental impact. The energy consumption required for mining and validating transactions on blockchain networks has been a growing concern, particularly for proof-of-work (PoW) consensus mechanisms used by some blockchain platforms like Bitcoin and Ethereum.

The energy consumption of PoW blockchains stems from the fact that miners must solve complex mathematical problems to validate transactions and add new blocks to the chain. This process requires a significant amount of computational power, which in turn requires a large amount of energy. As the value of the cryptocurrency being mined increases, so does the amount of energy consumed in the mining process.

According to a 2019 report by the University of Cambridge, Bitcoin mining alone consumes an estimated 121.36 TWh per year, which is equivalent to the energy consumption of the entire country of Argentina. As the popularity of blockchain technology continues to grow and more organizations adopt it, the environmental impact of the technology is likely to become more significant.

One potential solution to this challenge is the use of alternative consensus mechanisms that require less energy than PoW. For example, proof-of-stake (PoS) mechanisms rely on a network of validators who hold a stake in the network, rather than miners solving complex mathematical problems. PoS requires significantly less energy than PoW, making it a more environmentally friendly alternative.

Another approach to reducing the environmental impact of blockchain technology is the use of renewable energy sources to power mining operations. Some blockchain networks are already exploring this option, with companies like Soluna and Greenidge Generation building renewable energy-powered mining facilities.

In addition to the environmental impact of blockchain technology, there are also concerns about the social impact of mining activities. Mining operations often require a significant amount of resources, including land and water, which can have a negative impact on local communities and the environment.

Overall, addressing the environmental impact of blockchain technology is an important ethical and social challenge that must be addressed as the technology continues to be adopted by more organizations. By exploring alternative consensus mechanisms and renewable energy sources, the blockchain community can work towards minimizing the environmental impact of the technology while still reaping its benefits.

Implications for data privacy and surveillance

Blockchain technology has the potential to greatly impact data privacy and surveillance, both positively and negatively. On the one hand, blockchain can offer increased security and privacy protection for personal data by enabling secure and transparent data sharing without the need for intermediaries. On the other hand, it can also be used to facilitate surveillance and tracking of individuals, particularly in centralized blockchain systems.

One of the main challenges in the area of data privacy is the tension between the public nature of blockchain and the need for data privacy. Blockchain technology is inherently transparent and immutable, meaning that all transactions on the blockchain are public and cannot be altered or deleted. While this level of transparency can be beneficial in terms of accountability and trust, it can also raise concerns about privacy, particularly in cases where sensitive personal information is stored on the blockchain.

In addition, the use of smart contracts on the blockchain can also raise concerns about privacy and data protection. Smart contracts are self-executing contracts with the terms of the agreement directly written into code. While this can offer increased efficiency and automation, it can also create a potential for sensitive personal data to be stored on the blockchain, accessible to anyone with access to the blockchain network.

Moreover, the use of blockchain technology for surveillance purposes is also a significant concern. For example, centralized blockchain systems can be used to track and monitor individuals' behavior and transactions, which raises ethical questions about the potential abuse of this technology for surveillance and control purposes.

In order to address these challenges, there is a need for clear regulations and standards around data privacy and protection. This includes the need for clear consent mechanisms for the collection and use of personal data, as well as the development of privacy-preserving techniques and tools for blockchain systems. It is also important to ensure that blockchain technology is not used for unethical purposes, such as mass surveillance or tracking of individuals without their consent.

Another important consideration is the need for education and awareness-raising around the potential privacy implications of blockchain technology. This includes educating individuals on how their personal data may be used on the blockchain and the potential risks associated with this technology. This can help to promote informed decision-making around the use of blockchain technology and ensure that individuals are able to make informed choices about their data privacy.

In conclusion, while blockchain technology has the potential to greatly impact data privacy and surveillance, it is important to address the potential risks and challenges associated with this technology. Clear regulations and standards, privacy-preserving techniques, and education and awareness-raising efforts can help to ensure that blockchain technology is used ethically and responsibly, without compromising on data privacy and protection.

Potential for discrimination and bias in smart contracts

Smart contracts are self-executing contracts that use computer code to automate the negotiation and execution of an agreement. They are a key feature of blockchain technology and have the potential to revolutionize the way businesses and individuals transact with one another. However, as with any technology, there is the potential for smart contracts to perpetuate and exacerbate existing societal issues, such as discrimination and bias.

1. Understanding Bias in Smart Contracts

Smart contracts operate based on pre-defined rules that are encoded into the software. These rules are designed to execute a specific set of actions automatically when certain conditions are met. However, the way in which these rules are formulated and the data that is used to inform them can lead to bias and discrimination.

For example, if a smart contract is designed to automatically approve or deny loan applications based on certain criteria, such as credit score, income level, and employment history, the data used to inform these criteria may perpetuate existing biases and discrimination. For instance, if the historical data used to inform the smart contract's decision-making process contains biases, such as racial or gender-based discrimination, the smart contract will perpetuate these biases, resulting in discriminatory outcomes.

2. Challenges in Addressing Bias in Smart Contracts

Addressing bias in smart contracts is challenging for several reasons. Firstly, the data used to inform the smart contract's decision-making process may contain biases that are difficult to detect and correct. Secondly, the rules encoded into the smart contract may be difficult to modify once they have been deployed, making it challenging to correct for biases in real-time.

Additionally, there may be challenges in determining who is responsible for addressing bias in smart contracts. Smart contracts are typically decentralized and do not have a single entity responsible for their operation. This can make it difficult to determine who is accountable for addressing bias and discrimination.

3. Implications for Society

The potential for discrimination and bias in smart contracts has significant implications for society. Smart contracts have the potential to automate many aspects of daily life, including employment, housing, and financial transactions. If biases and discrimination are perpetuated through these automated systems, it can exacerbate existing power imbalances and further marginalize already vulnerable populations.

For instance, if a smart contract perpetuates gender-based discrimination in employment decisions, it can perpetuate existing inequalities and limit opportunities for women in the workforce. Similarly, if a smart contract perpetuates racial biases in housing decisions, it can further marginalize already vulnerable populations.

4. Addressing Bias in Smart Contracts

Addressing bias in smart contracts requires a multi-pronged approach. Firstly, there needs to be a concerted effort to ensure that the data used to inform smart contract decision-making processes is free from biases and discrimination. This may require the development of new data collection and analysis techniques that are designed to detect and correct for biases.

Secondly, there needs to be increased transparency and accountability in the development and deployment of smart contracts. This may require the development of new governance models that enable stakeholders to oversee the development and operation of smart contracts.

Finally, there needs to be increased education and awareness among stakeholders about the potential for bias and discrimination in smart contracts. This may involve training developers and other stakeholders in the ethical implications of smart contract development and operation.

Conclusion

Blockchain technology has the potential to revolutionize many industries and create a more decentralized, secure, and transparent future. However, it is not without its challenges, particularly in the areas of ethics and social responsibility. As discussed in this chapter, the potential for blockchain technology to exacerbate existing power imbalances, compromise data privacy, facilitate discrimination and bias, and harm the environment must be carefully considered and addressed.

To mitigate these challenges, it is crucial that stakeholders take a proactive and collaborative approach to the development and implementation of blockchain solutions. This includes engaging with communities and groups affected by the technology, implementing robust privacy and security measures, ensuring transparency and accountability in decision-making processes, and designing smart contracts that are free from bias and discrimination.

Moreover, it is essential that ethical considerations are given as much weight as technical considerations in the design and implementation of blockchain systems. This requires a shift in mindset from a purely technological focus to one that recognizes the social and ethical implications of blockchain technology.

In conclusion, while blockchain technology holds immense promise for transforming industries and driving innovation, it is imperative that its development and implementation are guided by ethical principles and considerations of social responsibility. Only then can we realize the full potential of this technology in a way that benefits society as a whole.

Potential for environmental harm and inequality

Blockchain technology has been touted as a solution to many problems, including those related to environmental sustainability. However, like any other technology, it has its own set of environmental impacts that must be taken into consideration. Additionally, blockchain technology has the potential to exacerbate existing environmental and social inequalities. In this section, we will explore the potential for environmental harm and inequality in the context of blockchain technology.

1. Environmental Impacts of Blockchain Technology

Blockchain technology is often praised for its decentralized and transparent nature, which could potentially reduce the need for intermediaries and, in turn, reduce carbon emissions and energy consumption. However, the reality is more complex than that. The energy consumption required for the operation of blockchain technology, especially proof-of-work-based blockchains, has been criticized as being too high and unsustainable.

In a proof-of-work blockchain, nodes compete to solve complex mathematical problems to validate transactions and add them to the blockchain. This process, known as mining, requires massive amounts of computing power and energy consumption. The Bitcoin network, for example, currently consumes more energy than entire countries such as Argentina and Ukraine. The environmental impact of such energy consumption is significant, as it contributes to climate change and other environmental issues.

Another environmental impact of blockchain technology is e-waste. As blockchain technology relies heavily on electronic devices, such as computers and smartphones, the disposal of these devices can have negative environmental consequences. Electronic waste, or e-waste, is a growing problem globally, with many electronic devices being disposed of improperly, leading to pollution and potential health risks.

2. Social and Environmental Inequalities

The potential for environmental harm caused by blockchain technology is not distributed equally. Developing countries that rely heavily on fossil fuels and have limited access to renewable energy sources are disproportionately affected by the energy consumption required for blockchain technology. These countries may also lack the resources and infrastructure necessary to dispose of e-waste properly, leading to further environmental harm.

In addition to environmental impacts, blockchain technology also has the potential to exacerbate existing social and economic inequalities. The high energy consumption required for mining can make it difficult for individuals or small organizations with limited resources to participate in the network. This could lead to a concentration of power and resources in the hands of a few, creating further inequalities.

Moreover, blockchain technology is not immune to human bias and discrimination. The development of smart contracts and algorithms that underlie blockchain technology can reinforce existing biases and discrimination. For example, if a smart contract is programmed to discriminate against certain groups, such as racial or gender minorities, the use of blockchain technology could further exacerbate social inequalities.

3. Addressing Environmental and Social Inequalities

Addressing the potential for environmental harm and social inequalities caused by blockchain technology requires a multi-faceted approach. One possible solution is the adoption of more energy-efficient consensus mechanisms, such as proof-of-stake or proof-of-authority, which require significantly less energy consumption than proof-of-work. Another solution is to encourage the development of renewable energy sources to power blockchain technology.

To address social inequalities, efforts must be made to ensure that blockchain technology is accessible to all, regardless of their economic or social status. This could involve the development of decentralized systems that allow for the participation of individuals and small organizations, as well as the implementation of anti-discrimination policies and regulations.

Furthermore, addressing the environmental and social impacts of blockchain technology requires collaboration and cooperation among various stakeholders, including governments, non-governmental organizations, and the private sector. By working together, it is possible to develop sustainable and equitable blockchain systems that benefit everyone.

Conclusion

The potential for blockchain technology to exacerbate environmental harm and inequality is a significant ethical and social challenge. While blockchain has the potential to create new opportunities for sustainable development and environmental conservation, it also poses risks to the environment and can worsen existing inequalities.

To address these challenges, it is important for blockchain developers, policymakers, and stakeholders to consider the environmental impact of blockchain projects and to design them in a way that promotes sustainability and reduces negative environmental externalities. This may involve using more energy-efficient consensus mechanisms, promoting the use of renewable energy sources, and incorporating environmental impact assessments into blockchain project planning and implementation.

Additionally, blockchain projects should consider the potential social and economic impacts of their implementation and strive to promote equity and fairness. This may involve ensuring that blockchain applications do not perpetuate existing inequalities or create new ones, and taking steps to address any potential negative impacts on vulnerable populations.

Overall, the ethical and social challenges associated with blockchain technology are complex and multifaceted. As the technology continues to evolve and gain widespread adoption, it will be important for stakeholders to work together to address these challenges and ensure that blockchain is used in a way that promotes sustainability, equity, and social welfare.

Potential for blockchain technology to facilitate unethical or illegal activities

While blockchain technology has the potential to bring many benefits and advancements to various industries, it is also important to consider its potential to facilitate unethical or illegal activities. The decentralized nature of blockchain makes it difficult to regulate and control, which can make it an attractive platform for those engaging in criminal activities. In this section, we will explore the potential for blockchain technology to facilitate unethical or illegal activities and the ethical implications of such activities.

1. Cryptocurrencies and illegal activities

One of the most prominent areas where blockchain technology has been associated with illegal activities is in the realm of cryptocurrencies. Cryptocurrencies, such as Bitcoin, have been used to facilitate illegal activities such as money laundering, tax evasion, and the purchase of illegal goods on darknet markets. The anonymity of transactions and the lack of regulation make it difficult to detect and prevent such activities. In addition, the use of cryptocurrencies for illegal activities can tarnish the reputation of blockchain technology and hinder its adoption in legitimate applications.

To address these concerns, many governments and regulatory bodies are increasing their efforts to regulate cryptocurrencies and prevent their use in illegal activities. For example, in the United States, the Financial Crimes Enforcement Network (FinCEN) has issued guidance on the use of cryptocurrencies for money laundering and other illegal activities. The guidance requires cryptocurrency exchanges and other virtual currency businesses to register with FinCEN and comply with anti-money laundering regulations.

2. Smart contracts and illegal activities

Another area where blockchain technology has the potential to facilitate illegal activities is in the use of smart contracts. Smart contracts are self-executing contracts with the terms of the agreement between buyer and seller being directly written into lines of code. While smart contracts can streamline and automate various processes, they can also be used to facilitate illegal activities, such as contract fraud, theft, and extortion.

One potential solution to address these concerns is to incorporate ethical considerations into the design and implementation of smart contracts. For example, smart contracts could be designed with ethical guidelines and principles in mind, such as transparency, accountability, and fairness. In addition, there could be legal and regulatory frameworks in place to ensure that smart contracts are used in a responsible and ethical manner.

3. Blockchain and illegal content

Blockchain technology can also be used to facilitate the distribution of illegal content, such as copyrighted material or child pornography. The decentralized and anonymous nature of blockchain transactions can make it difficult to track and prevent the distribution of such content. In addition, the use of blockchain technology for illegal content can further exacerbate existing social and ethical issues related to online content and privacy.

To address these concerns, various initiatives have been proposed to prevent the distribution of illegal content on blockchain platforms. For example, some blockchain platforms have implemented content filtering mechanisms to prevent the distribution of illegal content. In addition, legal and regulatory frameworks can be put in place to hold blockchain platforms accountable for the distribution of illegal content.

4. Ethical considerations

The potential for blockchain technology to facilitate unethical or illegal activities raises important ethical considerations. It is important for developers, users, and regulatory bodies to consider the potential ethical implications of blockchain technology and take steps to ensure that it is used in a responsible and ethical manner.

One potential solution is to incorporate ethical considerations into the design and development of blockchain technology. This can include designing blockchain platforms with ethical principles such as transparency, accountability, and fairness in mind. In addition, regulatory bodies can work to ensure that blockchain technology is used in a responsible and ethical manner through the implementation of legal and regulatory frameworks.

Another solution is to promote ethical awareness and education among users of blockchain technology. This can include providing information and resources to help users understand the ethical implications of their actions on blockchain platforms and encouraging responsible use of blockchain technology.

Ethical and social implications of blockchain-based supply chain traceability

Supply chains play a crucial role in the global economy, connecting suppliers, manufacturers, distributors, and retailers to ensure that products are produced and delivered to consumers efficiently and effectively. However, supply chains are often complex and opaque, with limited visibility into the origin and journey of products, making it difficult to ensure that they are produced ethically and sustainably.

Blockchain technology offers the potential to address this challenge by enabling transparent and immutable tracking of products throughout the supply chain. By using blockchain-based supply chain traceability, companies can track products from their origin to their final destination, ensuring that they are produced ethically, sustainably, and in compliance with relevant regulations.

While blockchain-based supply chain traceability offers significant benefits, it also raises important ethical and social implications that must be carefully considered.

1. Transparency and Accountability

One of the main benefits of blockchain-based supply chain traceability is increased transparency and accountability. By providing a tamper-proof and auditable record of product journey, blockchain can help to prevent fraud, counterfeiting, and other unethical practices that can occur throughout the supply chain.

However, this increased transparency also raises concerns about privacy and confidentiality. Some stakeholders may be hesitant to share sensitive information, such as proprietary production processes, with others in the supply chain. Additionally, the visibility provided by blockchain may expose previously unknown supply chain vulnerabilities, which could be exploited by bad actors.

To address these concerns, companies implementing blockchain-based supply chain traceability should establish clear policies around data privacy, confidentiality, and access control. Additionally, they should engage with all stakeholders in the supply chain to ensure that everyone understands the benefits and risks of using blockchain.

2. Fairness and Equity

Blockchain-based supply chain traceability can also help to promote fairness and equity by providing more transparent information about the conditions under which products are produced. This can help to prevent labor abuses and other unethical practices, ensuring that workers are treated fairly and paid a living wage.

However, the implementation of blockchain-based supply chain traceability may also exacerbate existing power imbalances within the supply chain. Small suppliers and producers may struggle to meet the technological and financial requirements necessary to participate in blockchain-based traceability programs, leading to further concentration of power in the hands of large companies.

To mitigate these risks, companies should work to ensure that blockchain-based traceability is accessible to all suppliers, regardless of their size or technological capabilities. Additionally, they should engage with suppliers and other stakeholders to ensure that everyone is aware of the benefits and risks of using blockchain, and that there is a shared understanding of how it will be implemented.

3. Sustainability and Environmental Impact

Blockchain-based supply chain traceability can also play a significant role in promoting sustainability and reducing the environmental impact of supply chains. By providing transparency about the environmental impact of production processes, companies can identify areas for improvement and work to reduce their carbon footprint.

However, the use of blockchain technology itself can also have an environmental impact. The energy-intensive nature of blockchain transactions, particularly for proof-of-work-based consensus mechanisms, can contribute to climate change and other environmental harms.

To address this concern, companies implementing blockchain-based supply chain traceability should consider using more energy-efficient consensus mechanisms, such as proof-of-stake or proof-of-authority. Additionally, they should work to reduce the overall energy consumption of their blockchain infrastructure by using renewable energy sources or implementing energy-saving measures.

Conclusion

Blockchain technology has the potential to transform various industries and improve efficiency, transparency, and security. However, it also presents a number of ethical and social challenges that must be addressed to ensure that its adoption benefits society as a whole. The issues related to data privacy and ownership, environmental impact, discrimination and bias, and the facilitation of unethical or illegal activities are some of the most pressing concerns associated with blockchain technology.

To overcome these challenges, stakeholders must take a proactive approach and work together to develop clear legal and regulatory frameworks that promote responsible and ethical use of the technology. This may include developing standards for data privacy and security, establishing clear guidelines for the use of smart contracts, and implementing measures to minimize the environmental impact of blockchain networks.

Furthermore, it is crucial to promote greater awareness and education around the ethical and social implications of blockchain technology. This may involve providing training and resources for developers and other professionals working in the blockchain space, as well as engaging with the wider public to promote greater understanding and discussion of the technology.

Ultimately, the responsible adoption and use of blockchain technology requires a collaborative effort from all stakeholders, including developers, regulators, businesses, and civil society organizations. By working together to address the ethical and social challenges associated with blockchain, we can harness the full potential of this innovative technology to create a more equitable and sustainable future for all.

Conclusion
Summary of key points

The use of blockchain technology has brought forth a range of benefits and challenges across various domains, including finance, legal, regulatory, and ethical. As highlighted in the preceding chapters, some of the most significant benefits of blockchain technology include decentralization, transparency, immutability, security, and efficiency. The technology has the potential to transform several industries, including finance, healthcare, logistics, and supply chain management, among others. However, the technology also poses numerous challenges that must be addressed to ensure its sustainable adoption and effective implementation.

One of the most significant challenges posed by blockchain technology is the regulatory and legal challenges. The lack of clear regulatory frameworks and guidelines has made it difficult for organizations to operate in a legally compliant manner, while the potential for cross-border transactions has raised concerns about international regulations. The technology's potential to facilitate illegal activities, such as money laundering and terrorism financing, has also been a major concern for regulators and law enforcement agencies.

Another critical challenge associated with blockchain technology is the ethical and social implications. The technology's potential to exacerbate existing power imbalances, such as wealth and income inequality, has raised concerns about its social impact. Additionally, the technology's potential for discrimination and bias in smart contracts has also been a significant concern, as has its potential for data privacy and surveillance.

Blockchain technology also poses significant challenges to achieving cost efficiencies and scale. The costs associated with blockchain implementation and maintenance, as well as the need for significant computing power, have made it challenging for organizations to realize the cost-saving benefits of the technology.

Finally, blockchain technology's potential environmental impact has also been a significant concern. The technology's high energy consumption and carbon footprint have raised concerns about its sustainability and its potential to exacerbate climate change.

Despite these challenges, blockchain technology remains a transformative technology with the potential to revolutionize several industries. By addressing the regulatory, legal, ethical, and environmental challenges, organizations can leverage the technology's benefits while mitigating its risks. However, this will require a collaborative effort from regulators, industry players, and other stakeholders to ensure that blockchain technology is implemented and used in an ethical, socially responsible, and sustainable manner.

In conclusion, the adoption of blockchain technology presents numerous opportunities and challenges across various domains, including finance, legal, regulatory, and ethical. While the technology has the potential to transform industries, it also poses significant challenges that must be addressed to ensure its effective implementation and sustainable adoption. Through collaborative efforts from stakeholders, these challenges can be addressed, and blockchain technology can be harnessed to create a more transparent, secure, and efficient future.

Strategies for mitigating the risks and challenges of adopting blockchain technology in supply chain management

As the use of blockchain technology in supply chain management continues to gain momentum, it is important for organizations to be aware of the potential risks and challenges associated with its adoption. In this section, we will discuss strategies for mitigating these risks and challenges.

1. Conduct a thorough risk assessment: Before adopting blockchain technology, organizations should conduct a comprehensive risk assessment to identify potential risks and challenges. This assessment should consider the potential impact of blockchain technology on the organization's existing processes, systems, and stakeholders. Based on the assessment, organizations can develop a plan to mitigate identified risks.

2. Develop a clear governance structure: A clear governance structure is essential to ensure the effective and efficient use of blockchain technology in supply chain management. This structure should clearly define the roles and responsibilities of all stakeholders involved in the use of blockchain technology, including suppliers, customers, and regulators.

3. Ensure compliance with legal and regulatory requirements: The legal and regulatory landscape surrounding blockchain technology is constantly evolving. Organizations should stay up-to-date on changes to regulations and ensure compliance with all relevant requirements. This may involve working with legal and regulatory experts to ensure that the use of blockchain technology is compliant with applicable laws and regulations.

4. Build trust and collaboration among stakeholders: The success of blockchain technology in supply chain management relies on trust and collaboration among stakeholders. Organizations should work to build trust with their suppliers, customers, and other stakeholders by providing transparent and

accurate information about their use of blockchain technology. Collaboration among stakeholders can help to ensure that the technology is being used in the most effective and efficient way possible.

5. Invest in education and training: Blockchain technology is complex and requires specialized knowledge and skills. Organizations should invest in education and training to ensure that their employees have the skills and knowledge needed to effectively use the technology. This may involve working with external experts or investing in internal training programs.

6. Monitor and evaluate the effectiveness of blockchain technology: It is important for organizations to monitor and evaluate the effectiveness of blockchain technology in their supply chain management processes. This can help to identify areas for improvement and ensure that the technology is being used in the most effective and efficient way possible.

In conclusion, the adoption of blockchain technology in supply chain management comes with both risks and rewards. By conducting a thorough risk assessment, developing a clear governance structure, ensuring compliance with legal and regulatory requirements, building trust and collaboration among stakeholders, investing in education and training, and monitoring and evaluating the effectiveness of the technology, organizations can mitigate the risks and challenges associated with its adoption and reap the benefits of increased efficiency, transparency, and security in their supply chain management processes.

Future outlook for blockchain technology in the supply chain

Blockchain technology has the potential to revolutionize supply chain management by increasing transparency, accountability, and efficiency. Despite the many challenges and risks associated with its adoption, organizations are increasingly exploring the use of blockchain in supply chain management. In this section, we will discuss the future outlook for blockchain technology in the supply chain, including emerging trends, opportunities, and challenges.

Emerging Trends One of the most significant emerging trends in the blockchain and supply chain space is the rise of hybrid blockchain networks. Hybrid blockchains offer the benefits of both private and public blockchains, providing organizations with greater flexibility and scalability. Hybrid blockchain networks can facilitate secure and efficient communication between different parties, allowing organizations to streamline their supply chain operations.

Another emerging trend is the integration of blockchain technology with the Internet of Things (IoT). IoT devices can generate vast amounts of data, which can be recorded and stored on a blockchain. This integration can enable organizations to track products and assets throughout the supply chain, providing them with real-time visibility and insights.

Opportunities Blockchain technology offers many opportunities for organizations to improve supply chain management. By providing a shared and immutable record of transactions, blockchain technology can increase transparency, traceability, and accountability throughout the supply chain. This can help organizations reduce the risk of fraud, counterfeiting, and other forms of supply chain-related risks.

Blockchain technology can also help organizations to streamline their supply chain operations by reducing the need for intermediaries and manual processes. By automating processes and eliminating intermediaries, organizations can reduce costs, increase efficiency, and improve their bottom line.

In addition, blockchain technology can facilitate the creation of new business models and revenue streams. By leveraging the benefits of blockchain technology, organizations can develop new products and services that are more efficient and cost-effective than traditional offerings.

Challenges While the potential benefits of blockchain technology in the supply chain are significant, there are still many challenges that must be addressed. One of the most significant challenges is the lack of standardization and interoperability between different blockchain networks. This can create significant barriers to adoption, particularly for organizations that are looking to collaborate with partners on different blockchain networks.

Another challenge is the scalability of blockchain technology. Blockchain networks can become slow and inefficient when they become congested, particularly when processing large volumes of transactions. This can limit the ability of organizations to use blockchain technology for high-volume applications.

Finally, there are significant legal and regulatory challenges associated with the use of blockchain technology in the supply chain. These challenges include data privacy, ownership, and liability, as well as compliance with international regulations.

Conclusion In conclusion, blockchain technology has the potential to transform supply chain management by increasing transparency, traceability, and efficiency. However, its adoption is not without challenges, and organizations must carefully consider these challenges before implementing blockchain solutions. To address these challenges, organizations must develop strategies for standardization, interoperability, scalability, and compliance. As the technology continues to evolve, it is likely that we will see new and innovative use cases for blockchain technology in the supply chain, and organizations that are able to leverage these opportunities will be well-positioned for success.

THE END

Potential References

Introduction:
Buterin, V. (2014). A next-generation smart contract and decentralized application platform. Ethereum White Paper, 1-32.
Swan, M. (2015). Blockchain: Blueprint for a new economy. O'Reilly Media, Inc.

Chapter 1: Technical Challenges:
Nakamoto, S. (2008). Bitcoin: A peer-to-peer electronic cash system.
Wood, G. (2014). Ethereum: A secure decentralised generalised transaction ledger. Ethereum Project Yellow Paper, 151.

Chapter 2: Security Challenges:
Tschorsch, F., & Scheuermann, B. (2016). Bitcoin and beyond: A technical survey on decentralized digital currencies. IEEE Communications Surveys & Tutorials, 18(3), 2084-2123.
Zohar, A. (2015). Bitcoin: Under the hood. Communications of the ACM, 58(9), 104-113.

Chapter 3: Organizational Challenges:
Crosby, M., Pattanayak, P., Verma, S., & Kalyanaraman, V. (2016). Blockchain technology: Beyond bitcoin. Applied Innovation, 2(6-10), 71-81.
Tapscott, D., & Tapscott, A. (2016). Blockchain revolution: how the technology behind bitcoin is changing money, business, and the world. Penguin.

Chapter 4: Financial Challenges:
Kshetri, N. (2018). Blockchain's roles in meeting key supply chain management objectives. International Journal of Information Management, 39, 80-89.
Swan, M. (2015). Blockchain: Blueprint for a new economy. O'Reilly Media, Inc.

Chapter 5: Legal and Regulatory Challenges:
Antonopoulos, A. M. (2014). Mastering bitcoin: Unlocking digital cryptocurrencies. O'Reilly Media, Inc.
Werbach, K. (2018). The blockchain and the new architecture of trust. MIT Press.

Chapter 6: Ethical and Social Challenges:
De Filippi, P., & Loveluck, B. (2016). The invisible politics of Bitcoin: governance crisis of a decentralised infrastructure. Internet Policy Review, 5(3), 1-25.
Hileman, G., & Rauchs, M. (2017). Global blockchain benchmarking study. Cambridge Centre for Alternative Finance, University of Cambridge.
Conclusion:
Crosby, M., Pattanayak, P., Verma, S., & Kalyanaraman, V. (2016). Blockchain technology: Beyond bitcoin. Applied Innovation, 2(6-10), 71-81.
Tapscott, D., & Tapscott, A. (2016). Blockchain revolution: how the technology behind bitcoin is changing money, business, and the world. Penguin.

www.ingramcontent.com/pod-product-compliance
Lightning Source LLC
LaVergne TN
LVHW012120070526
838202LV00056B/5808